50 PATTERNS
Coloring Book for Kids

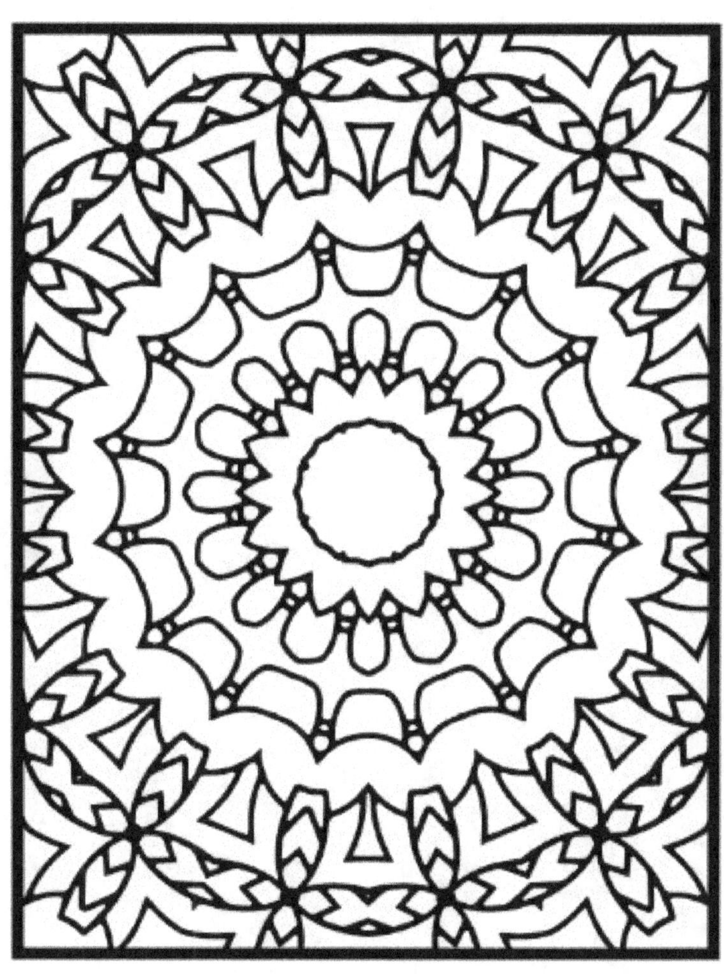

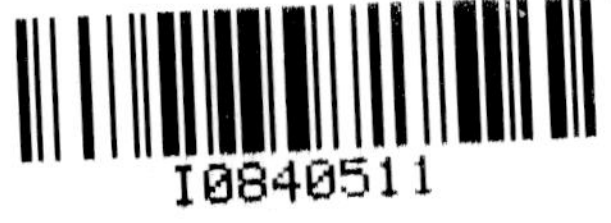

THIS BOOK BELONGS TO:

____

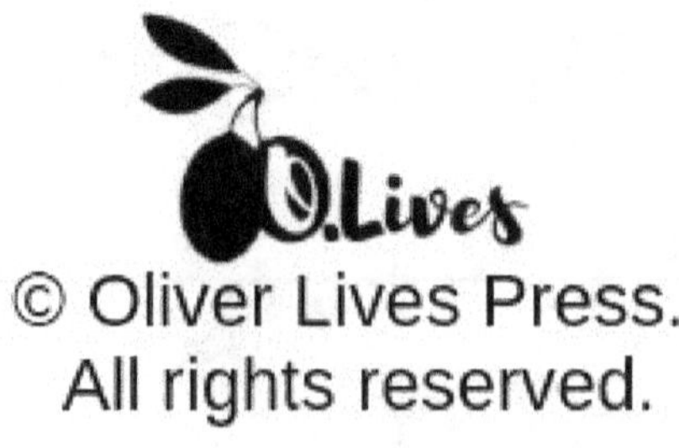

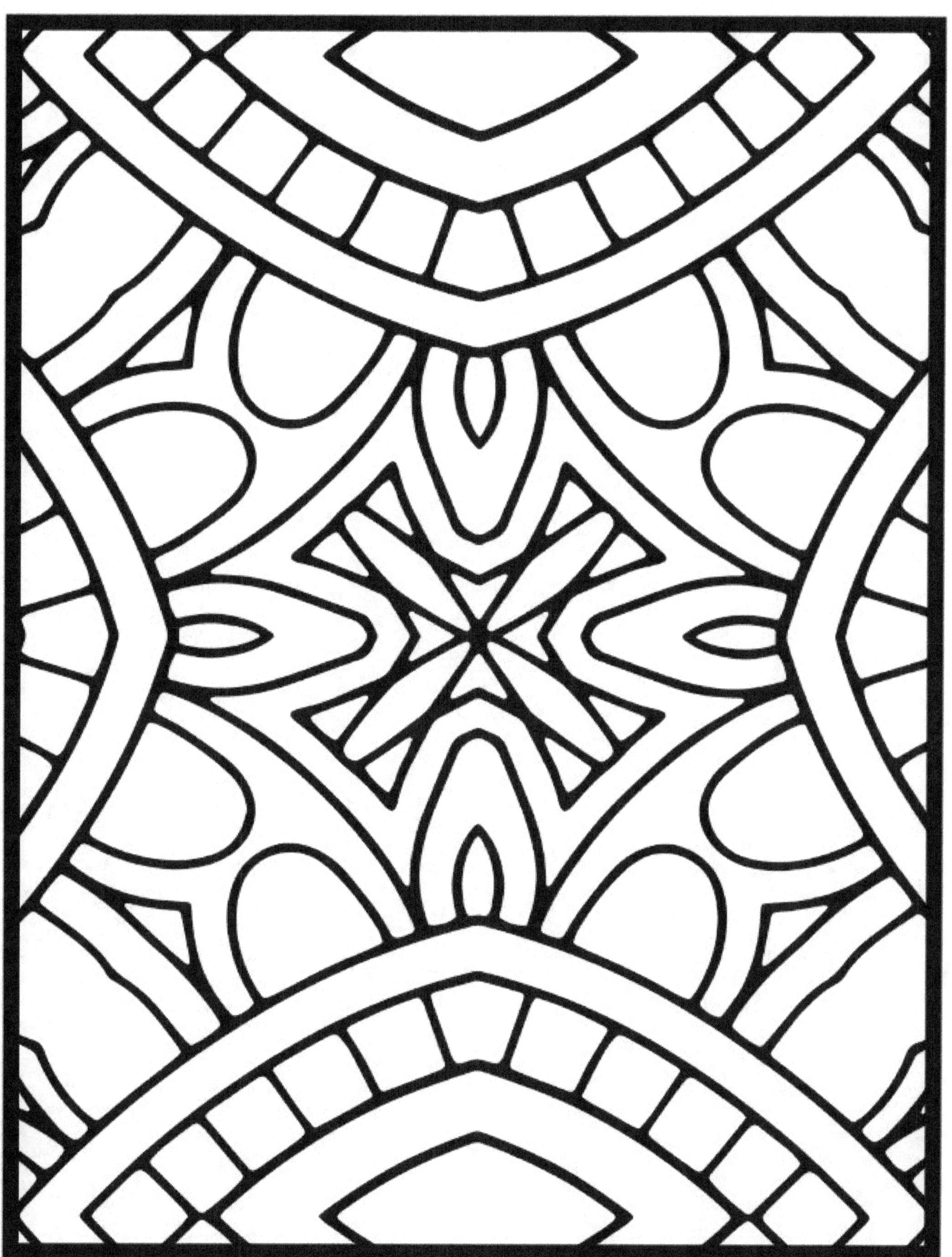

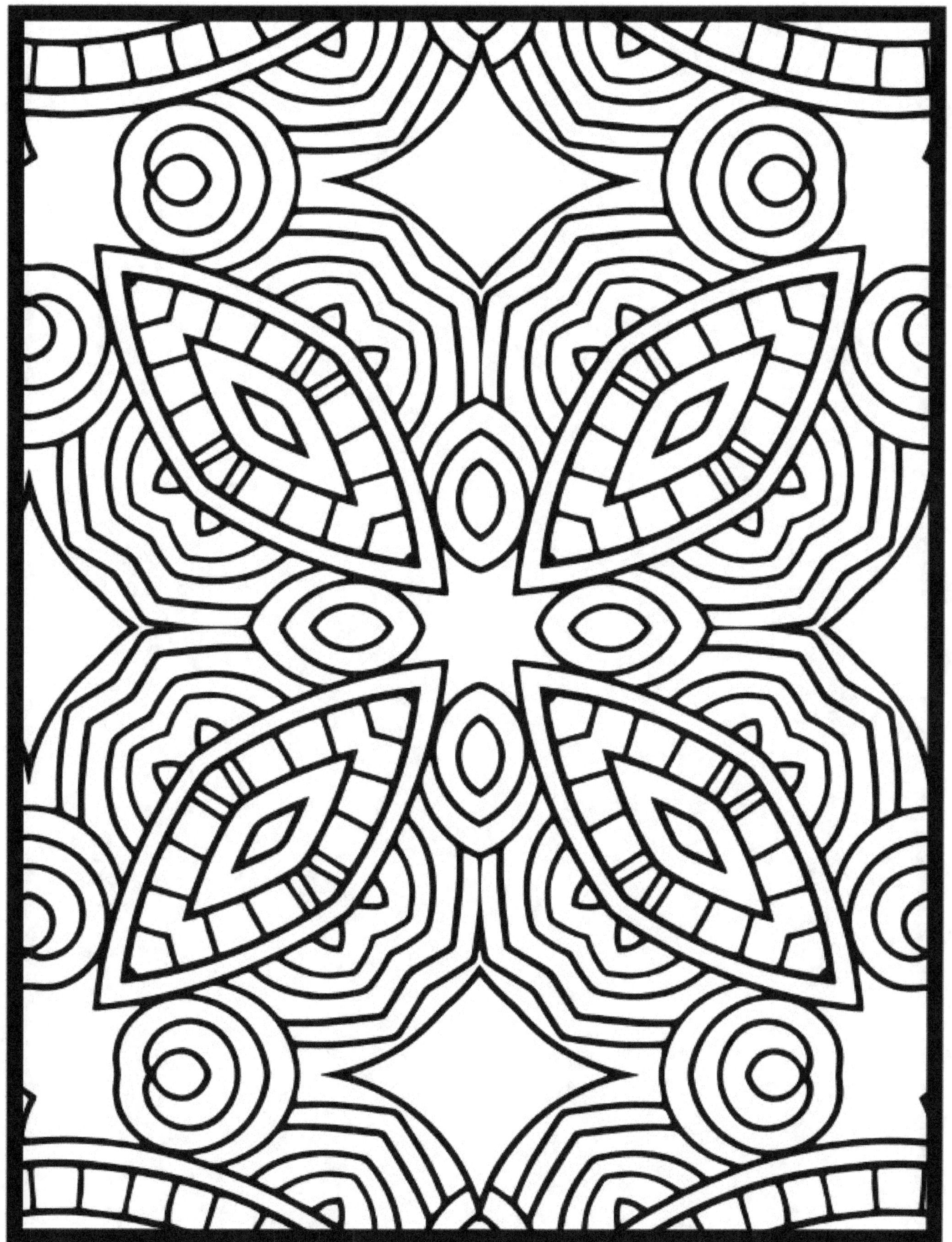

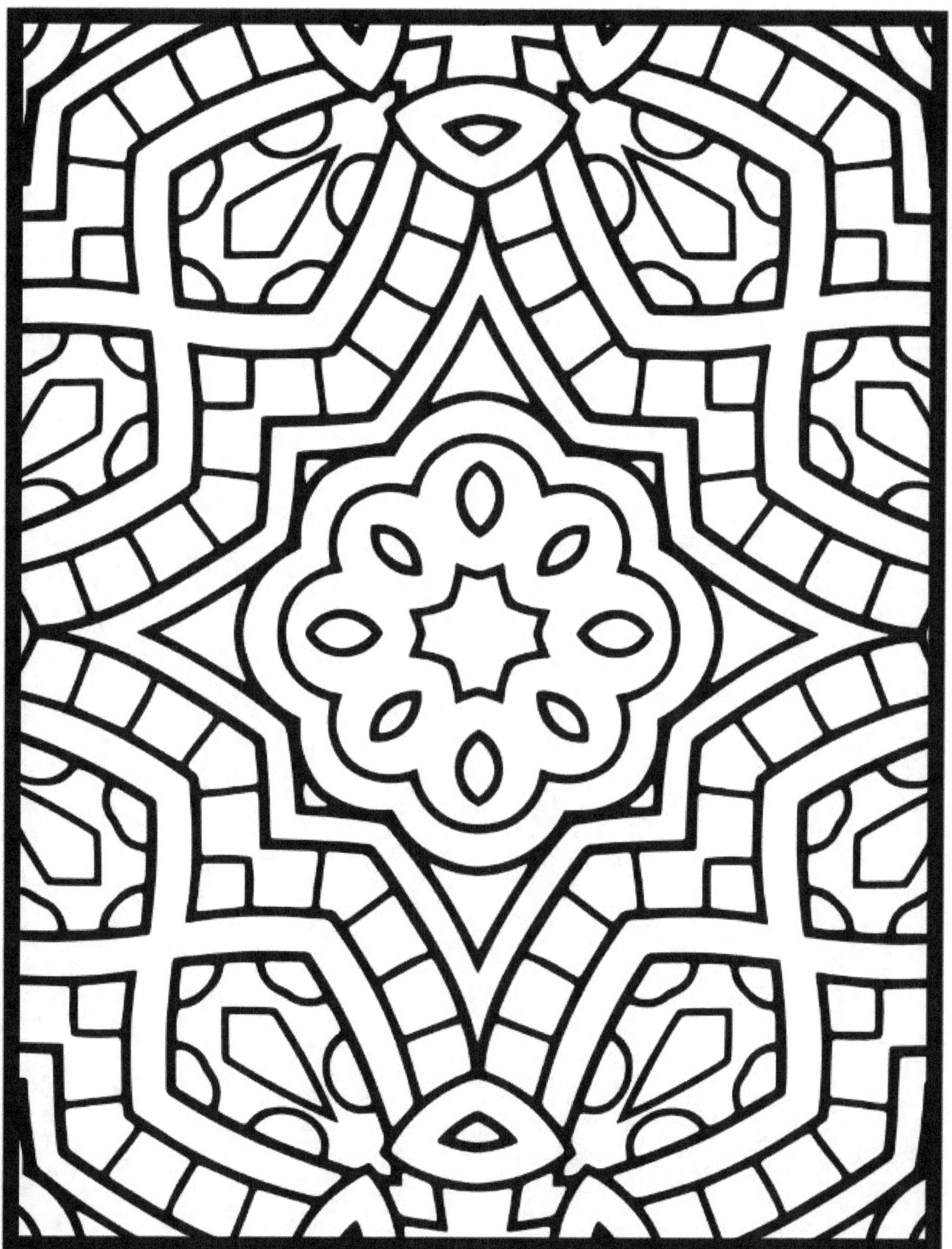

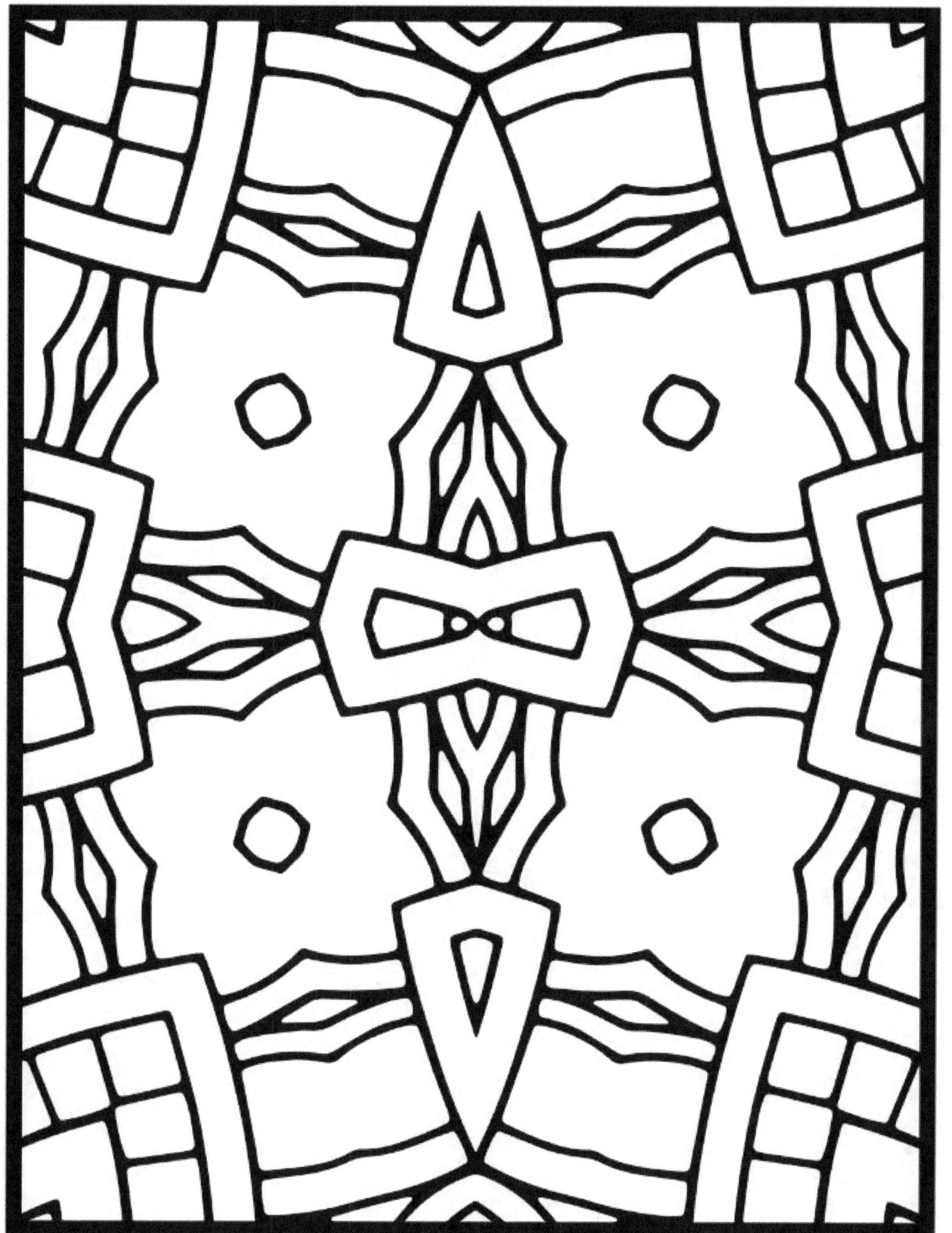

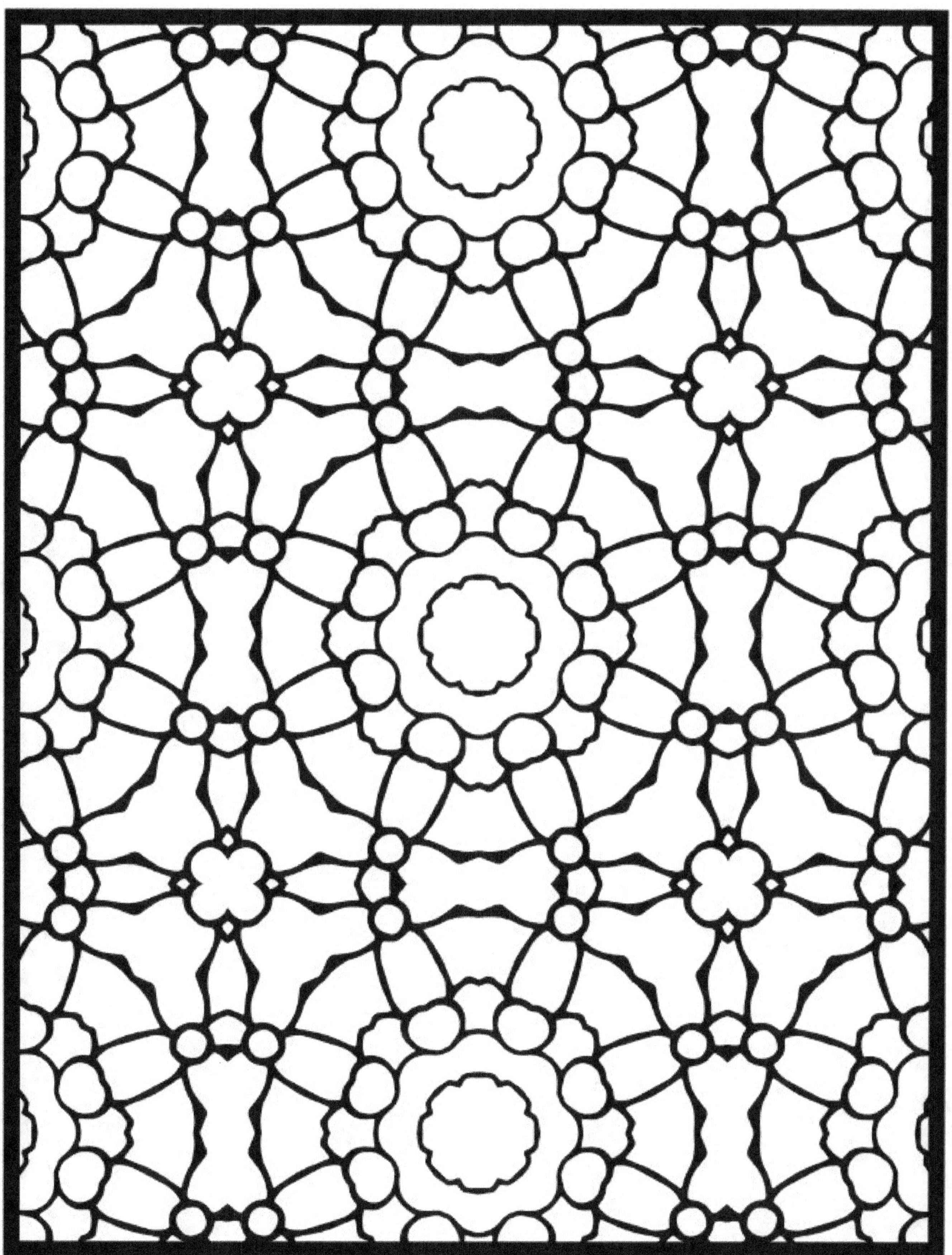

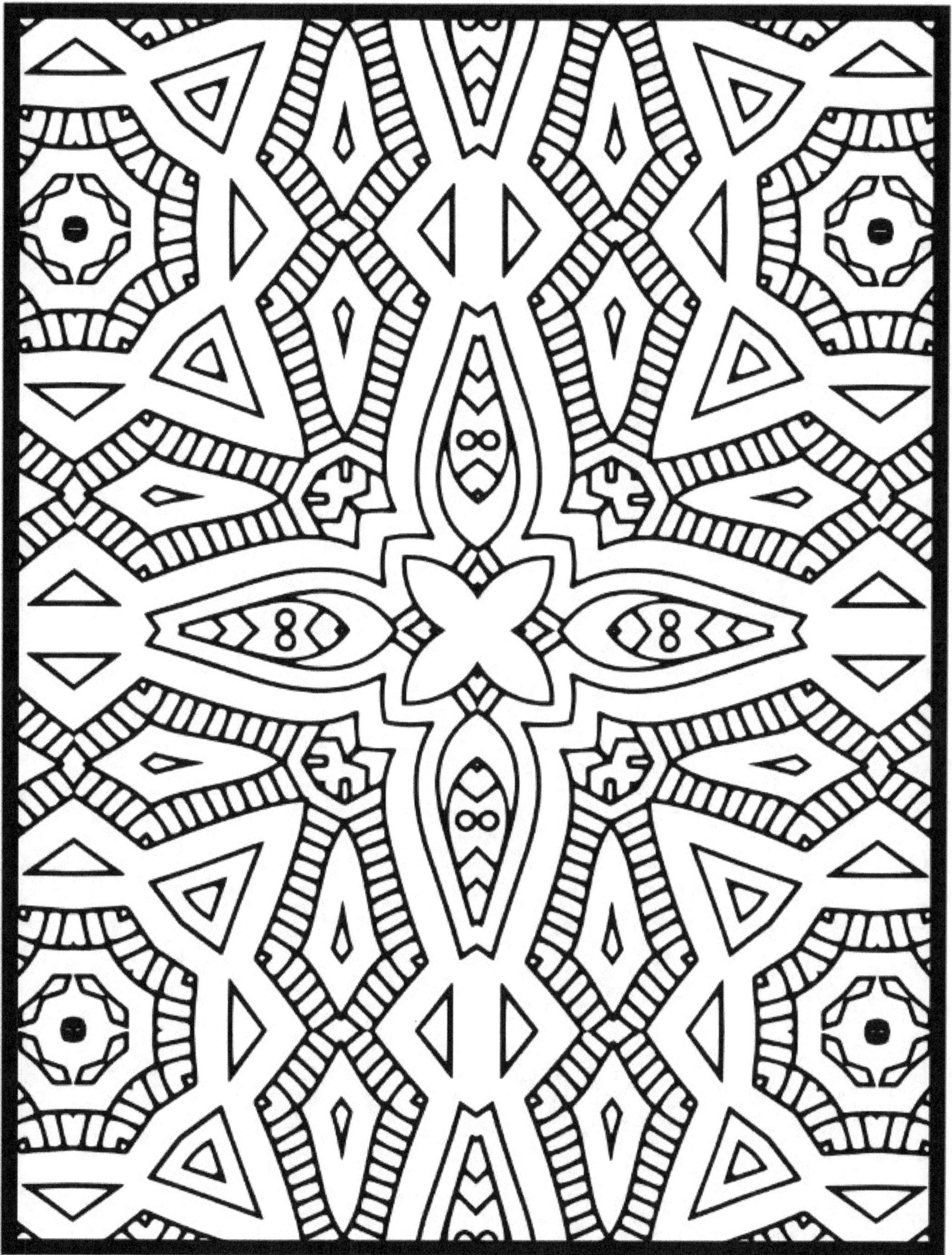

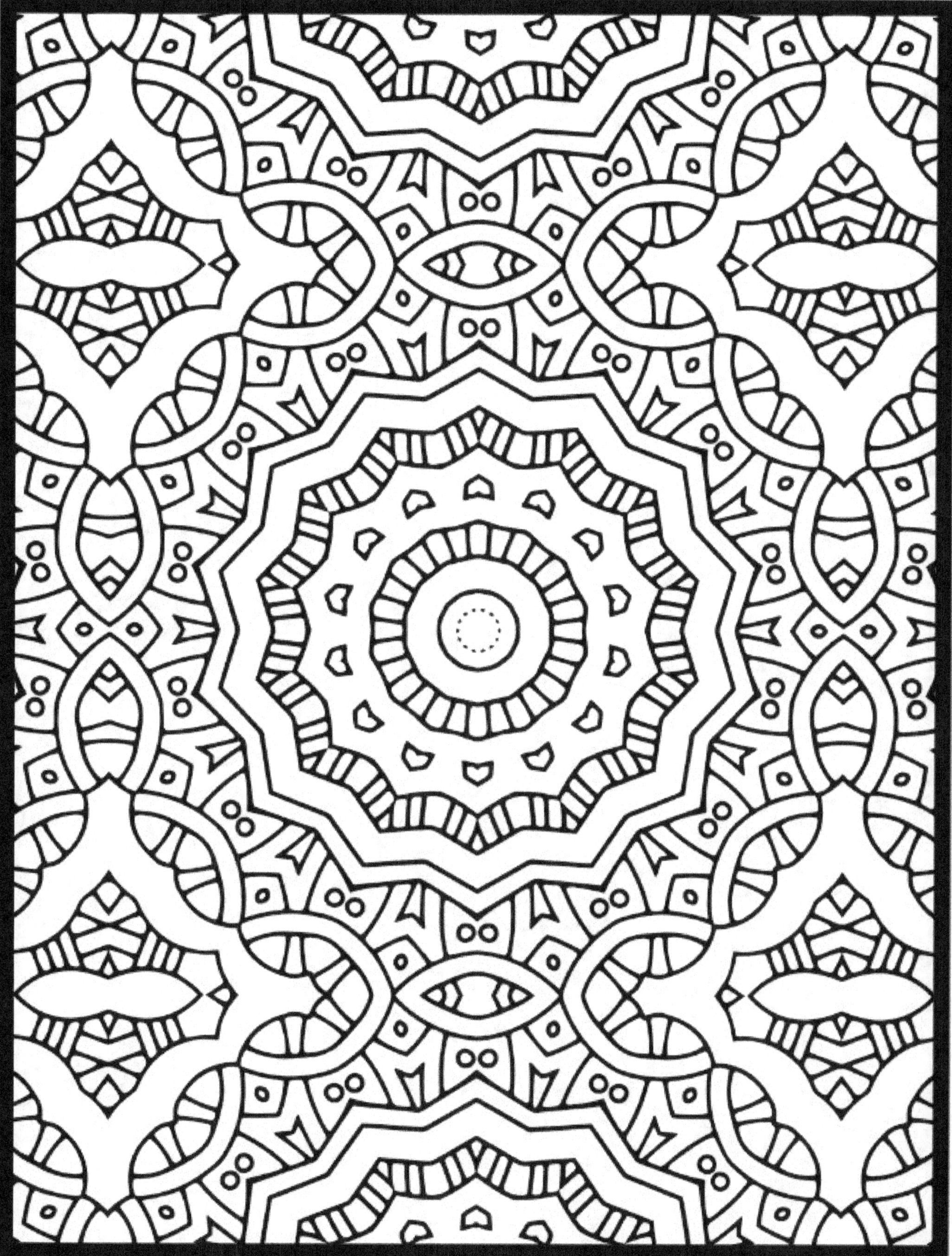

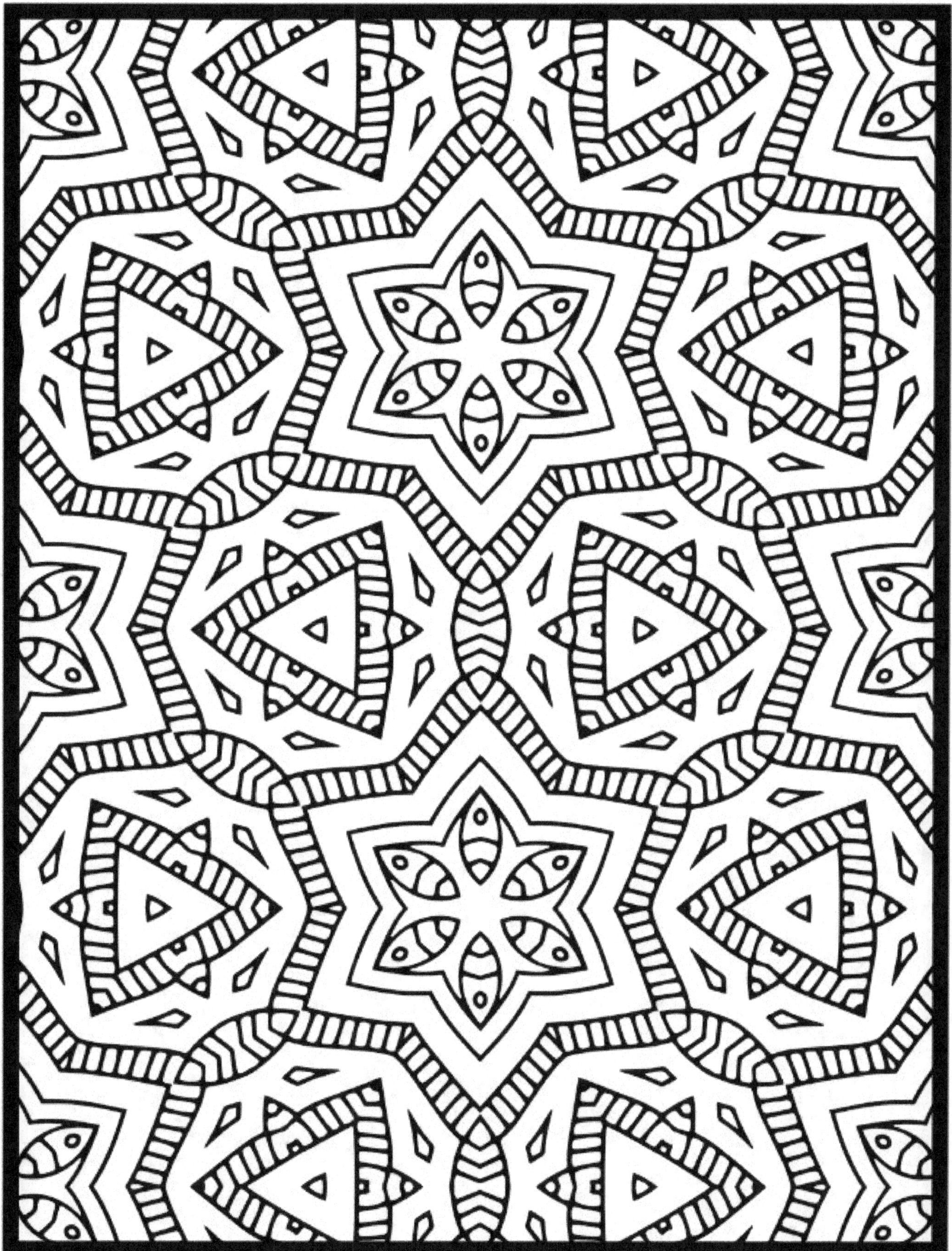

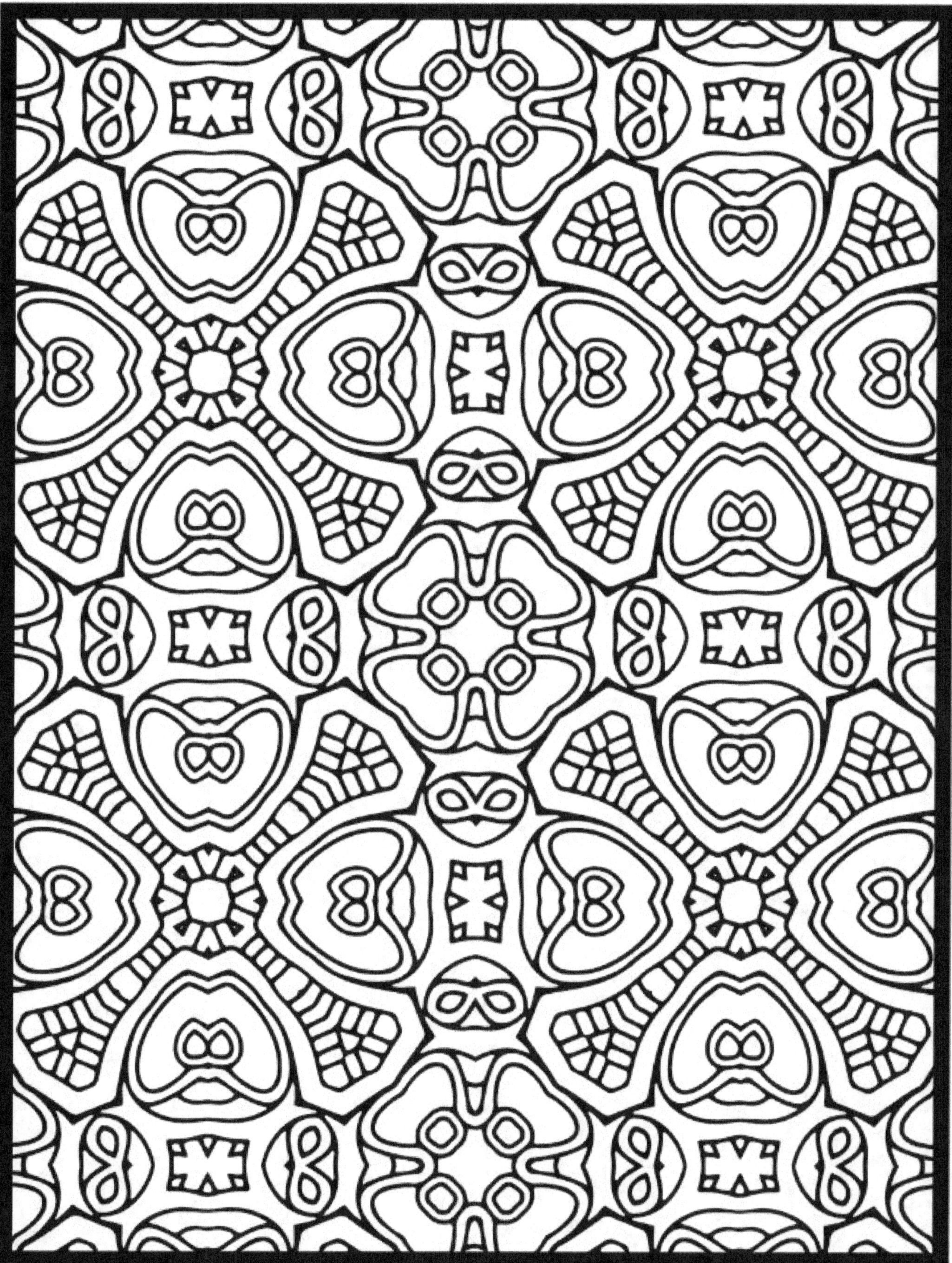

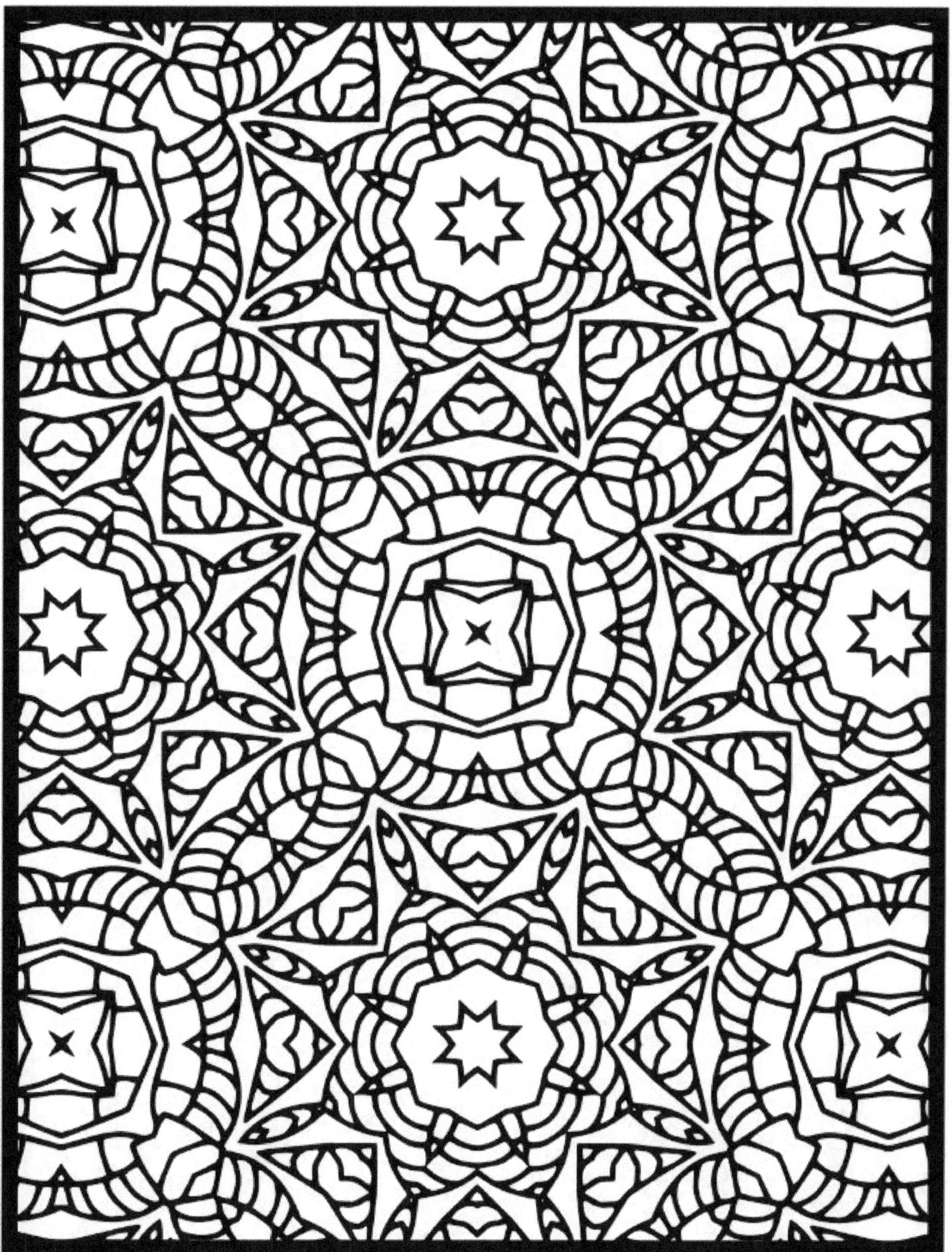

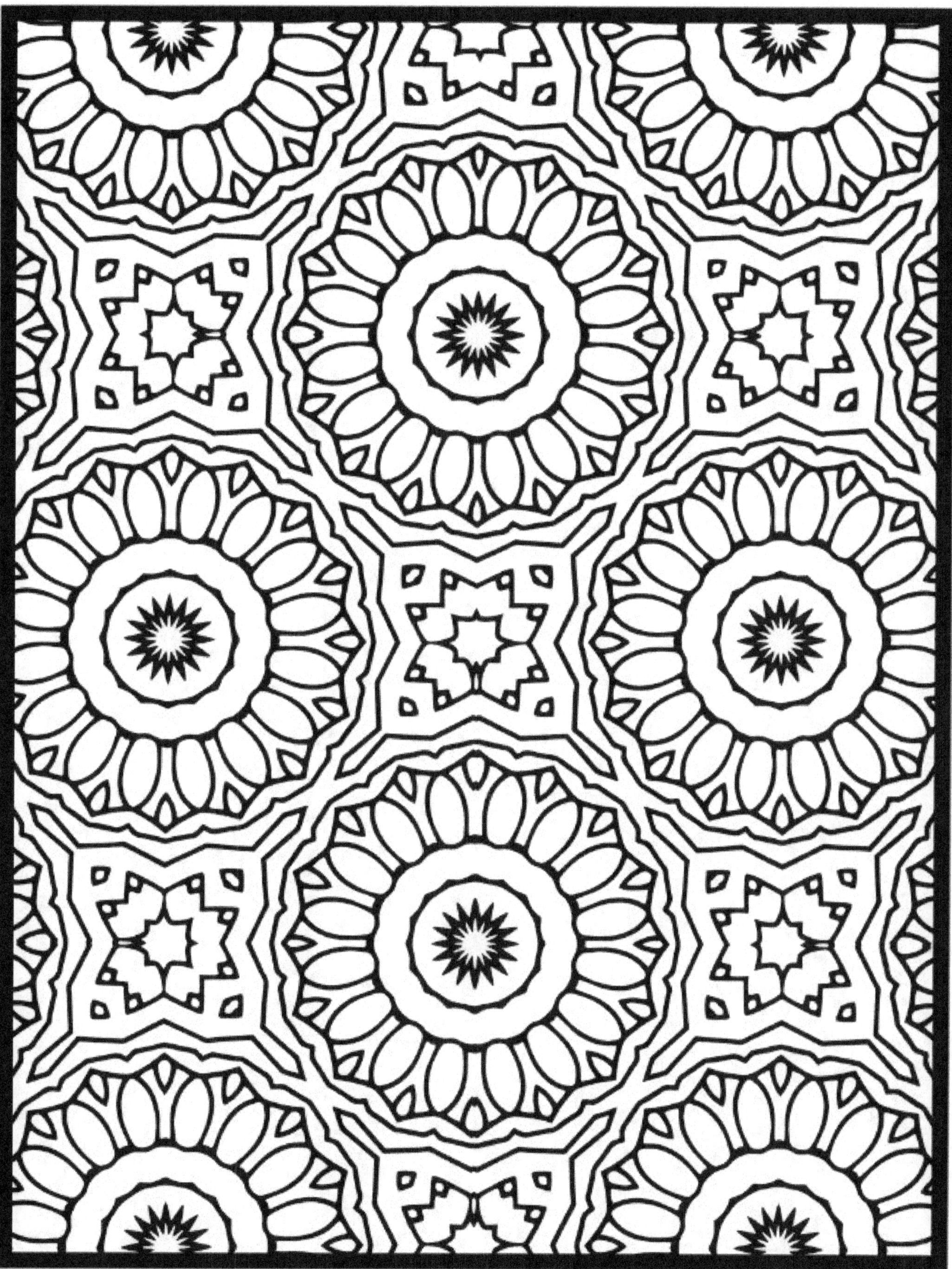

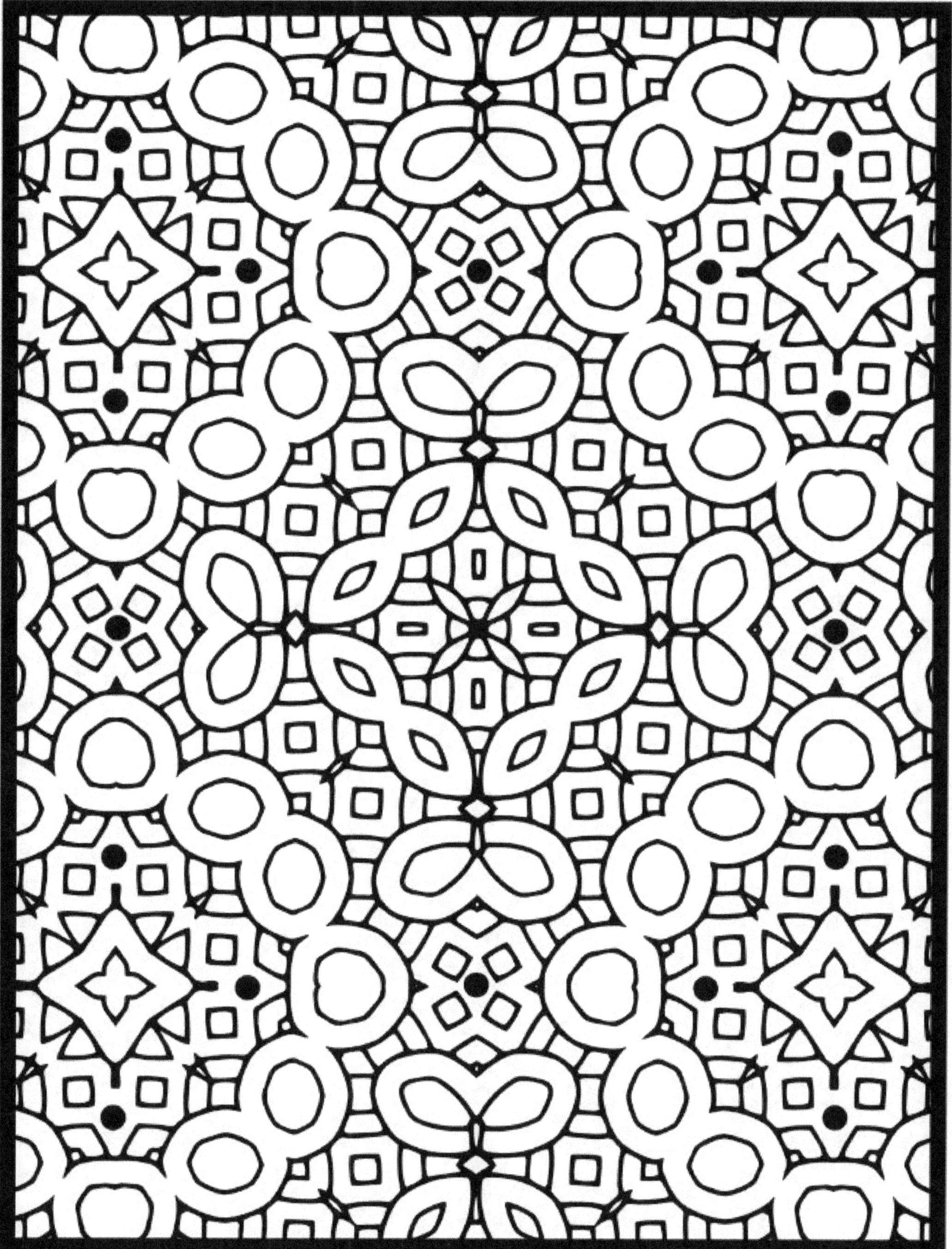

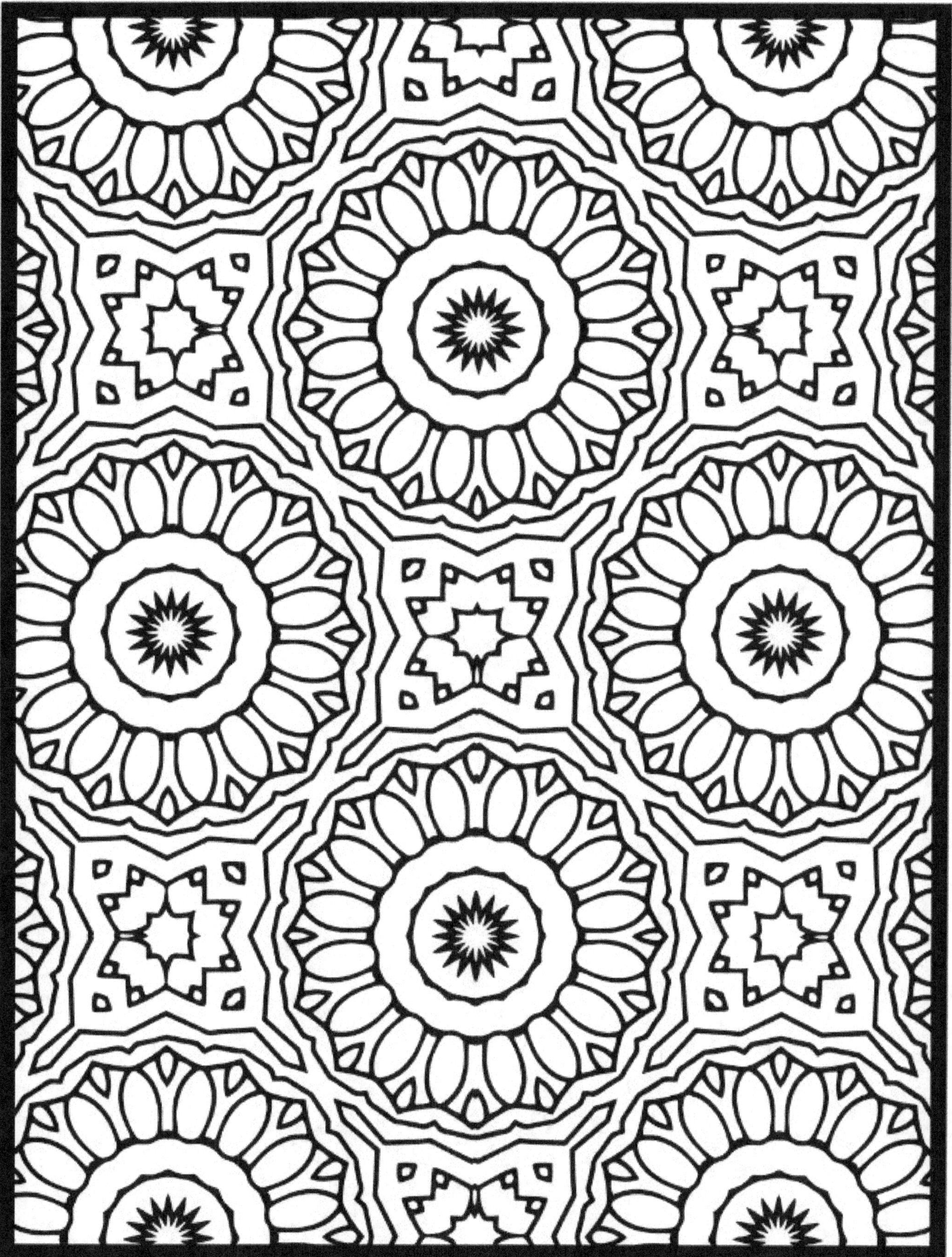

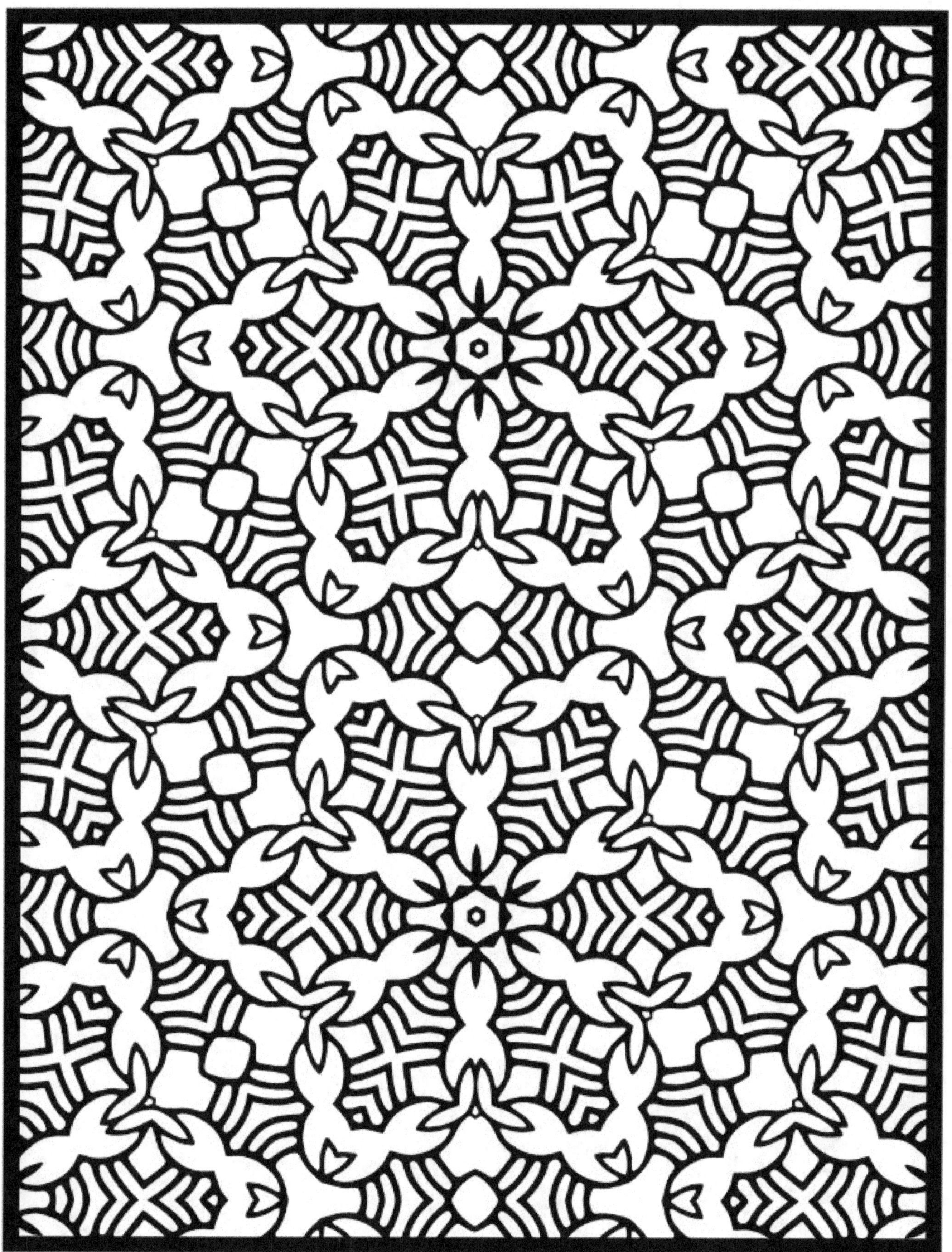

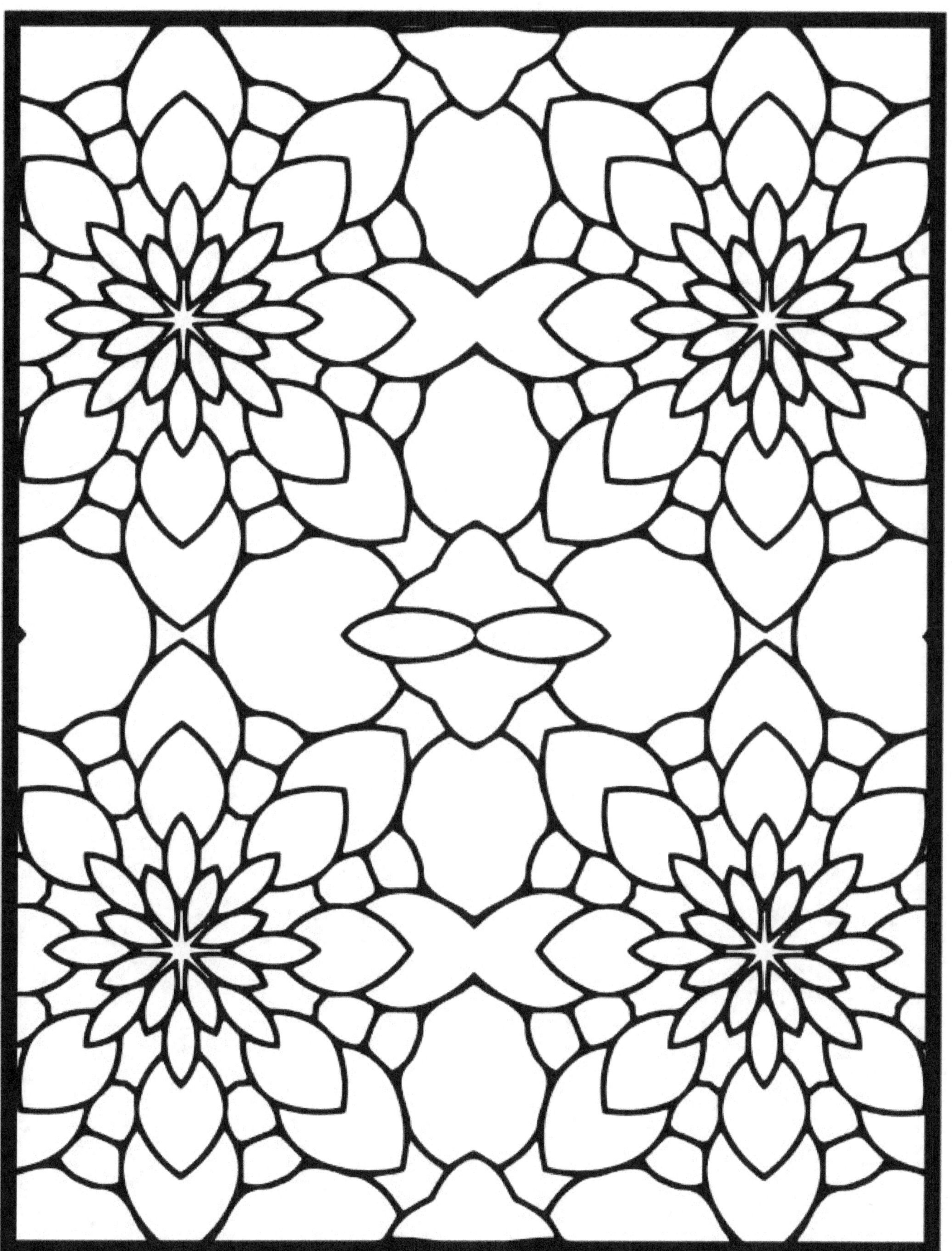

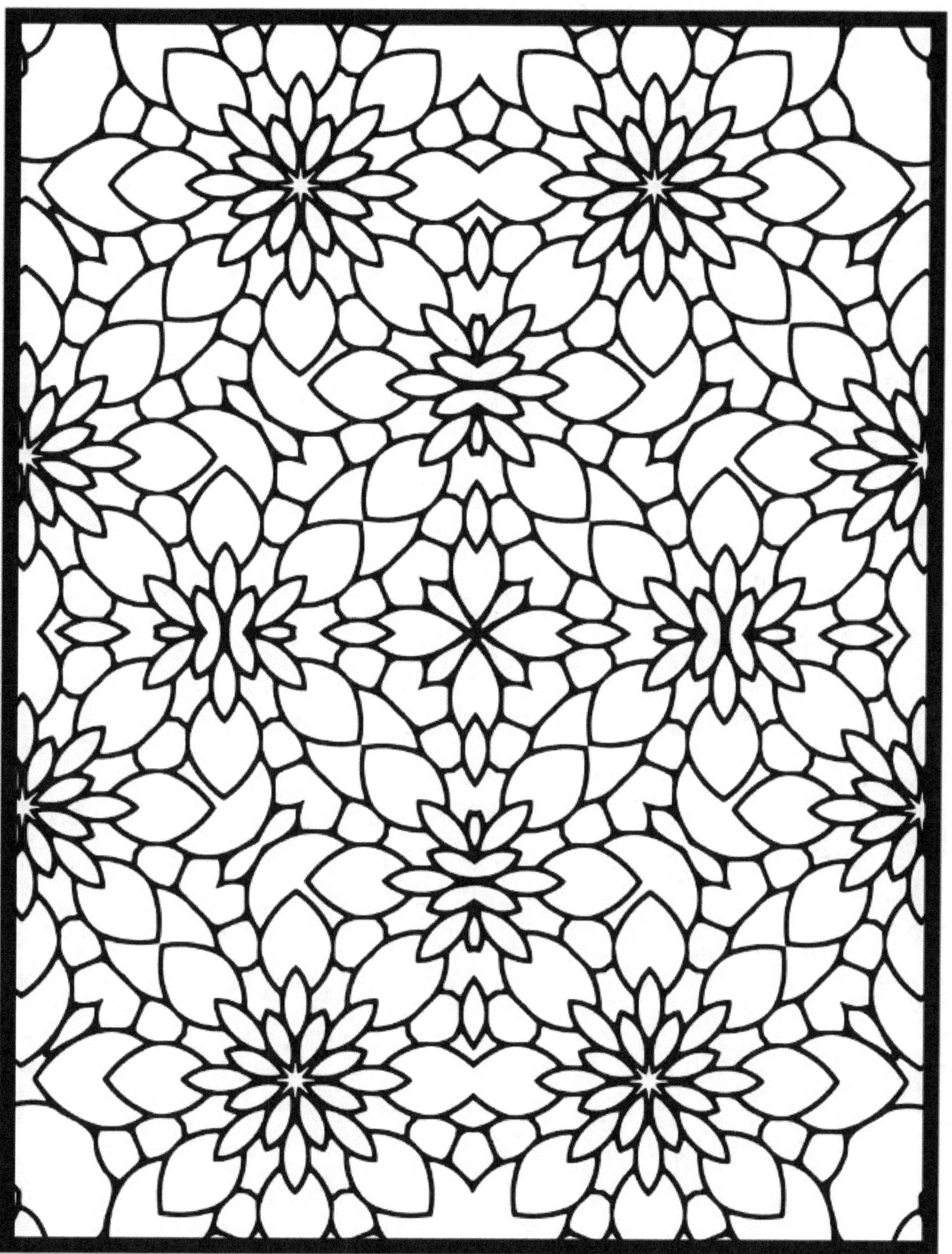

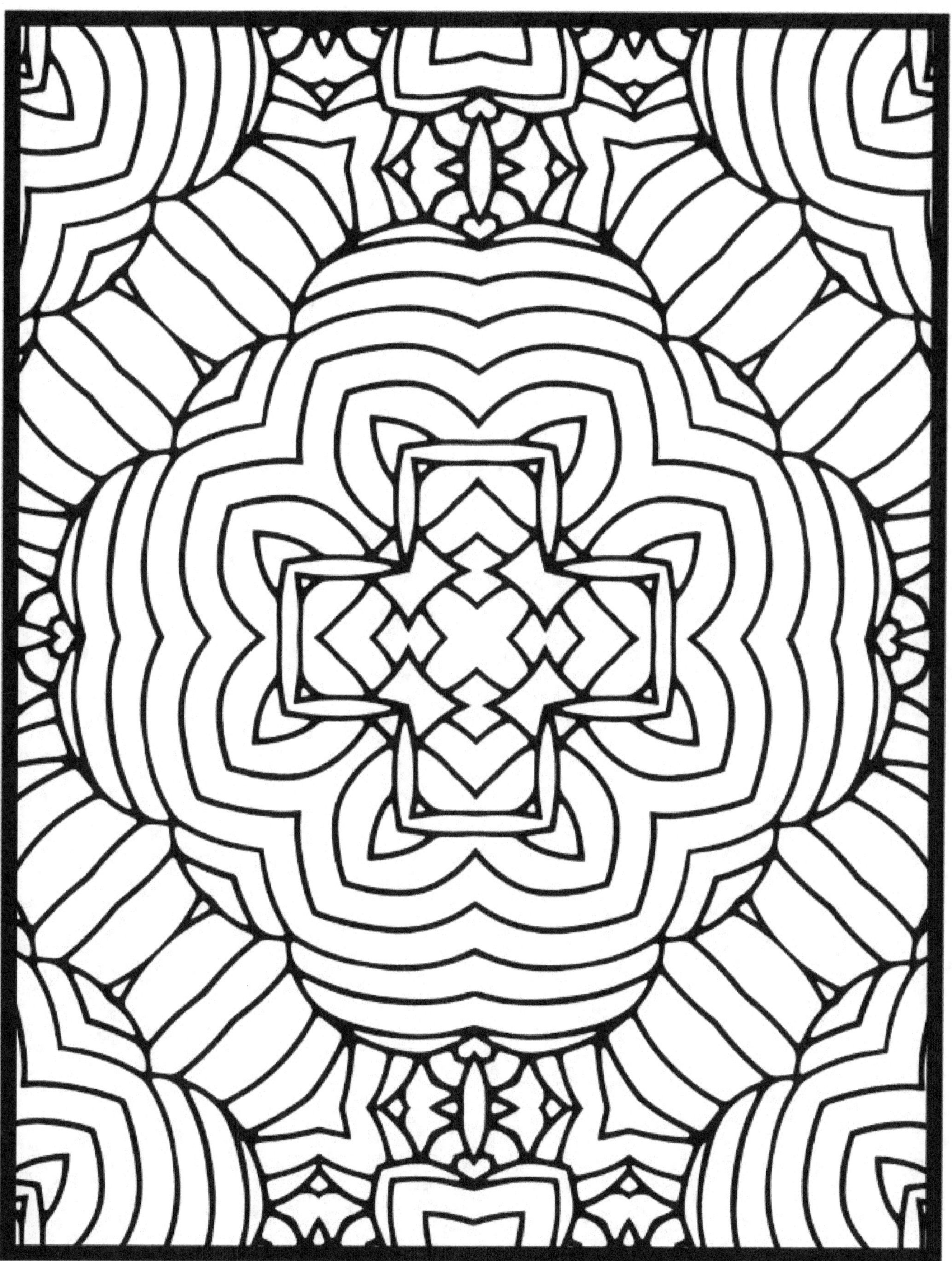

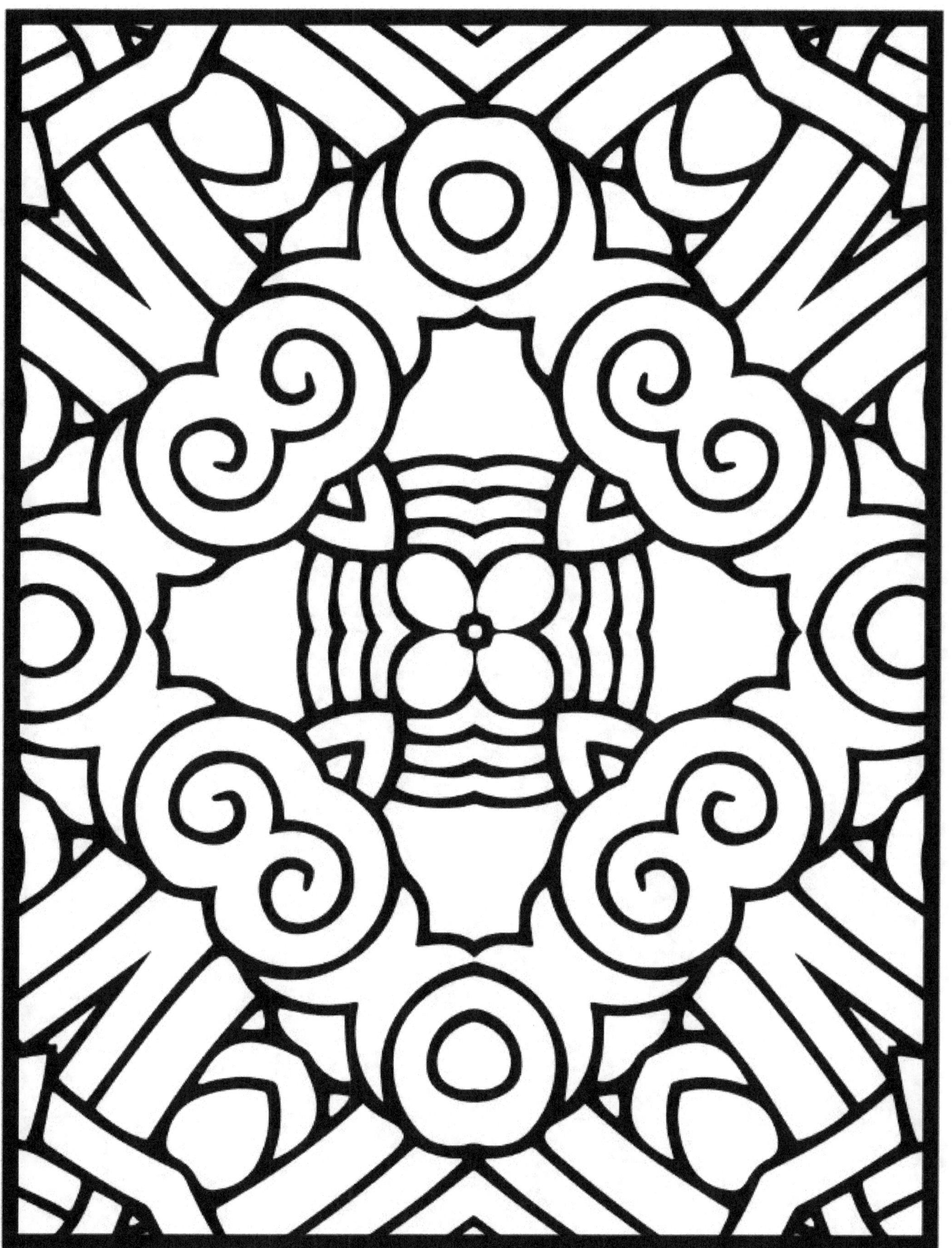

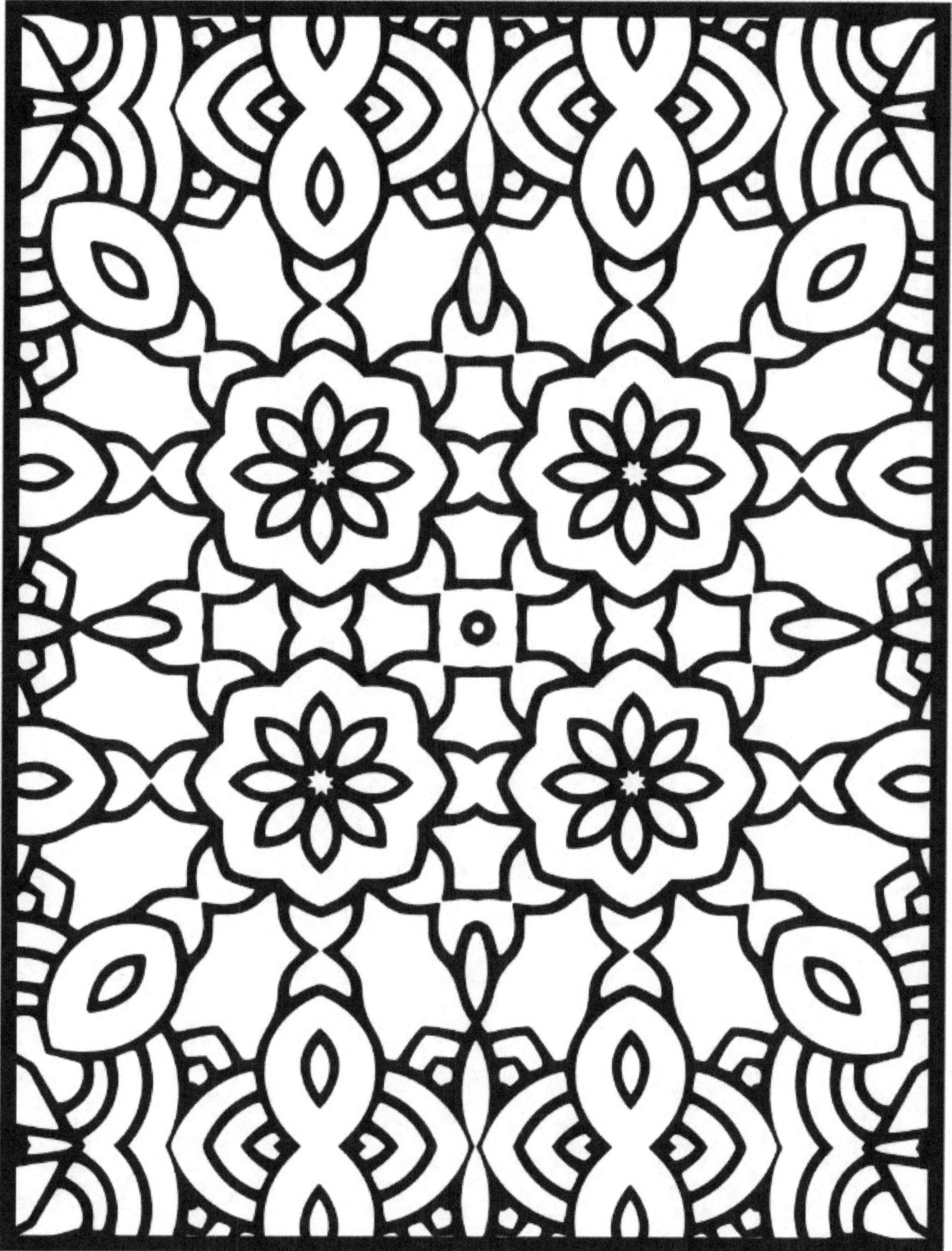

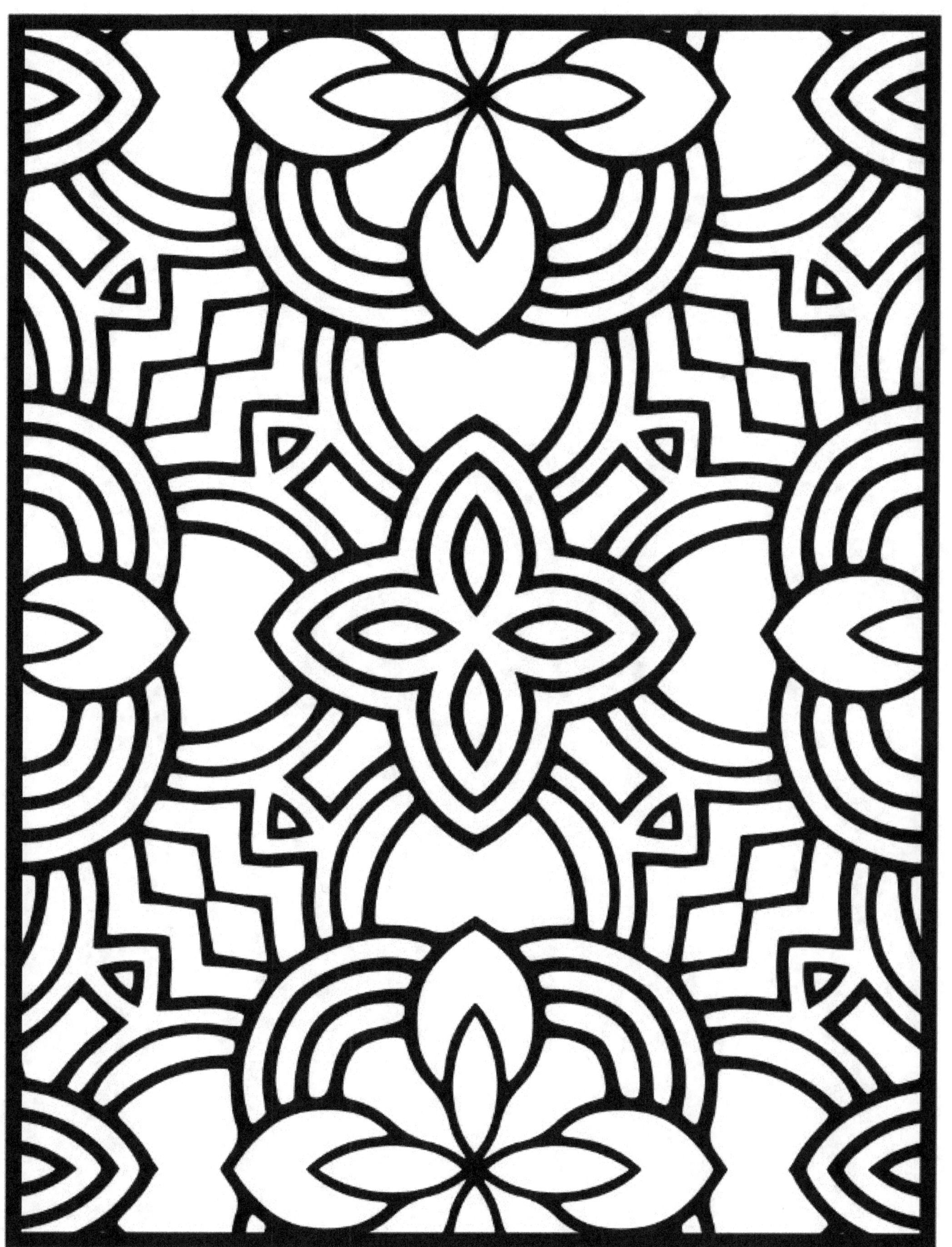

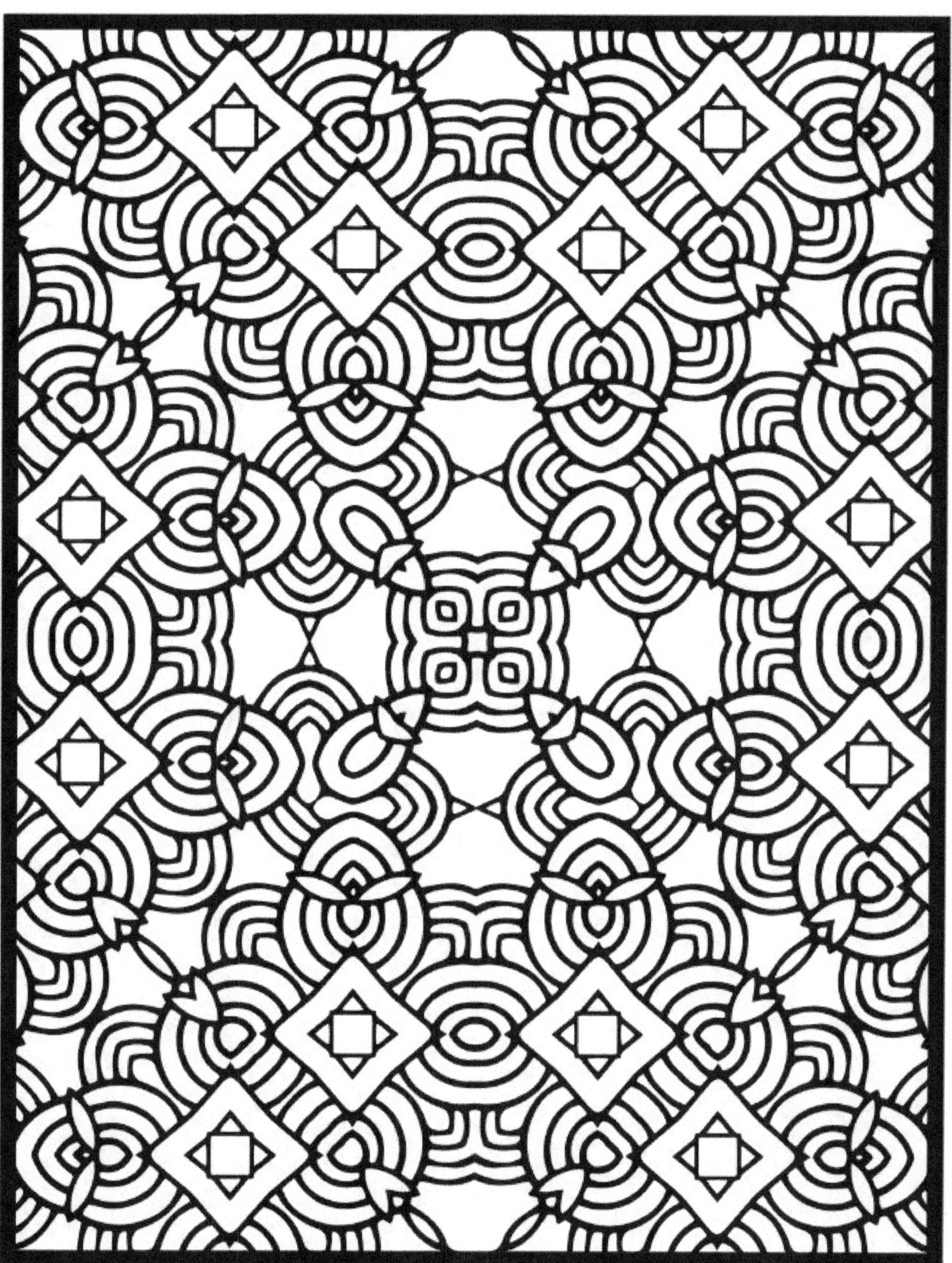

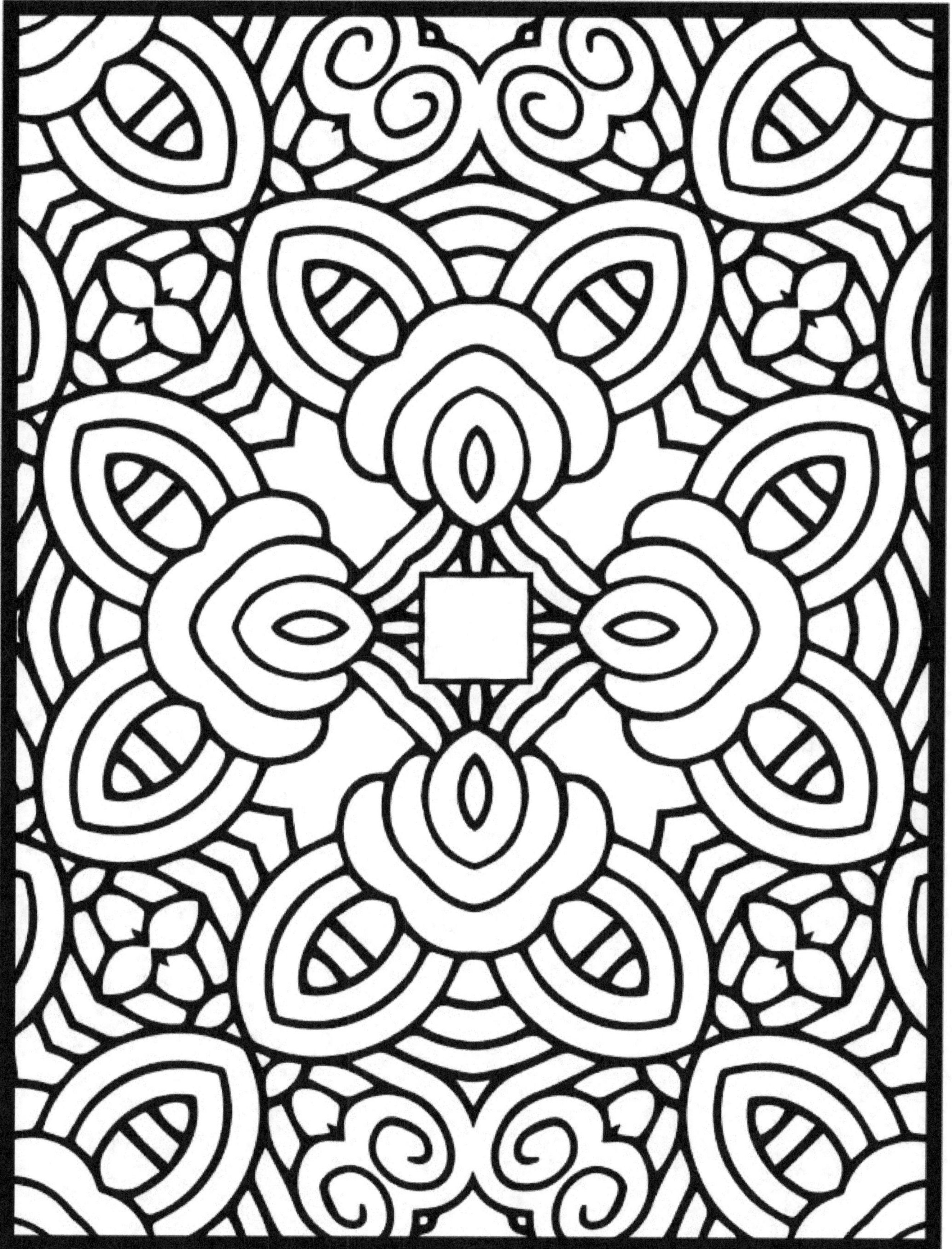

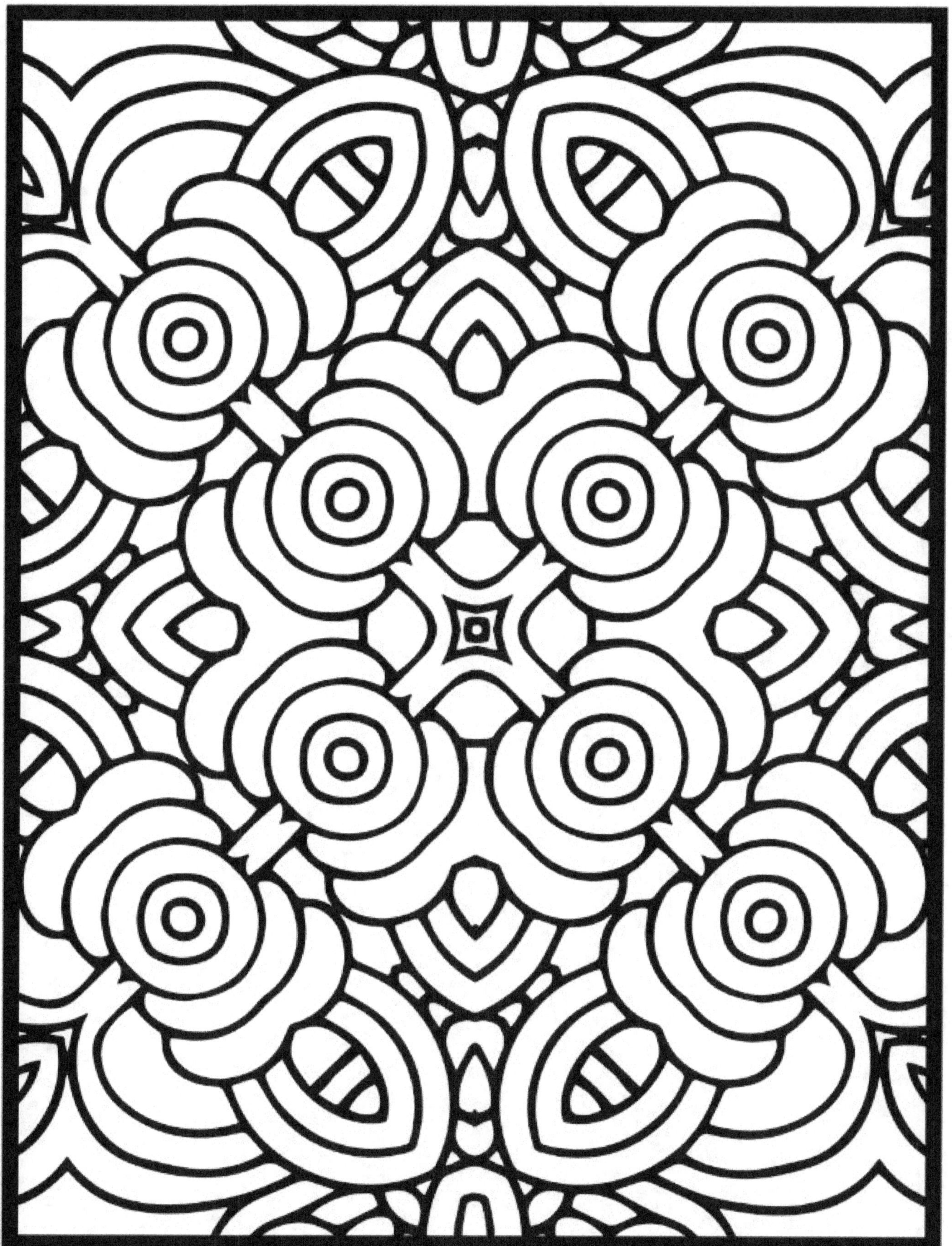

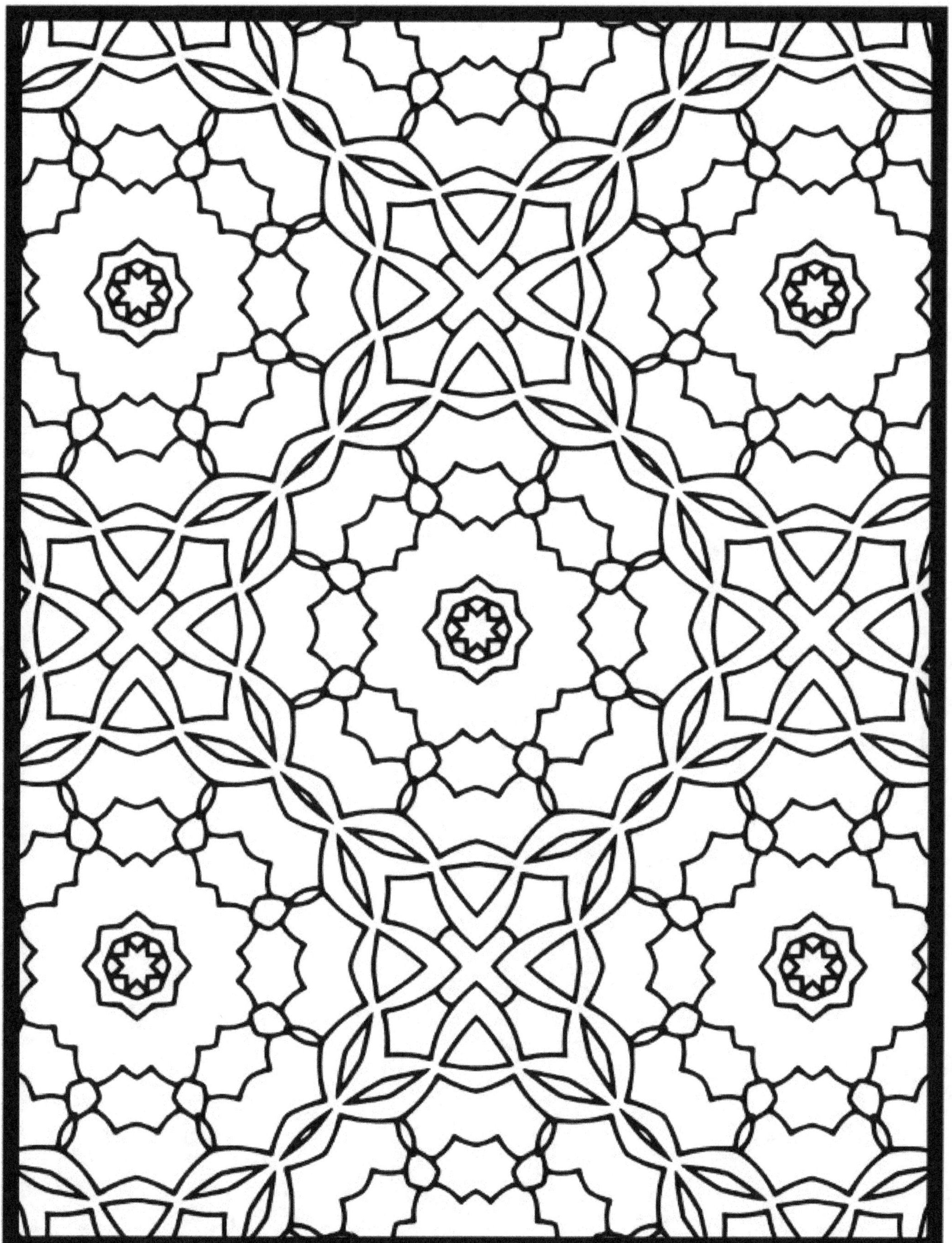

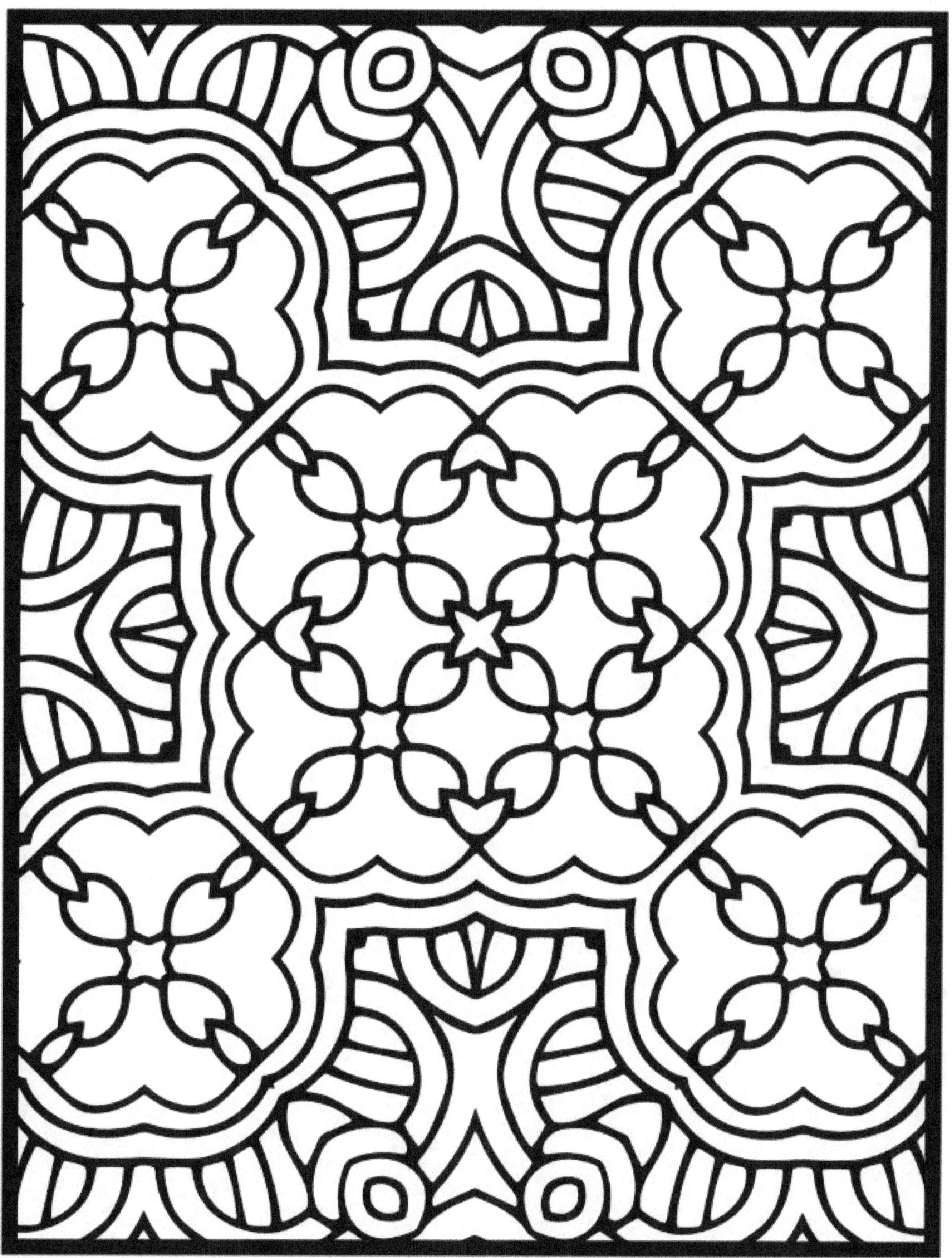

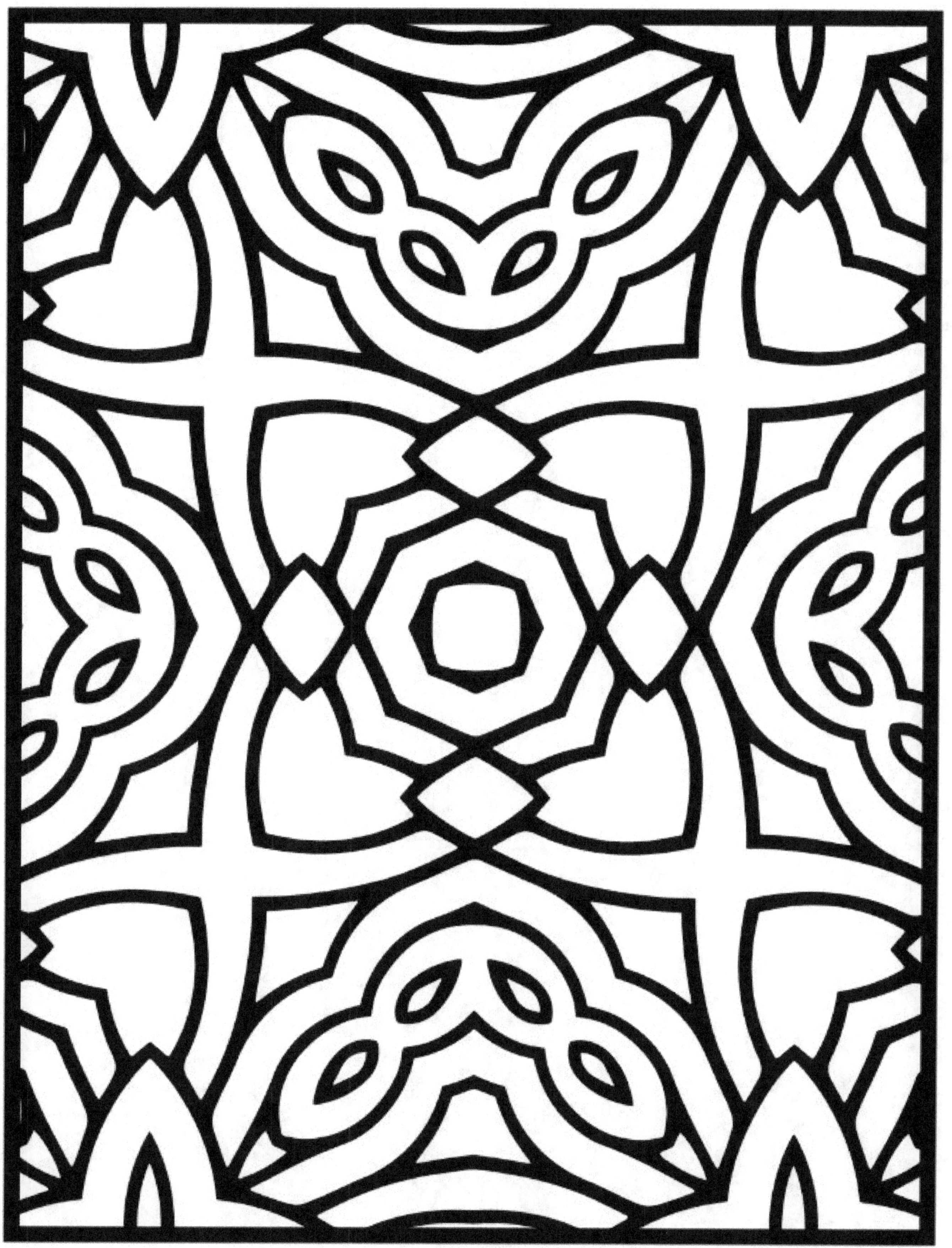

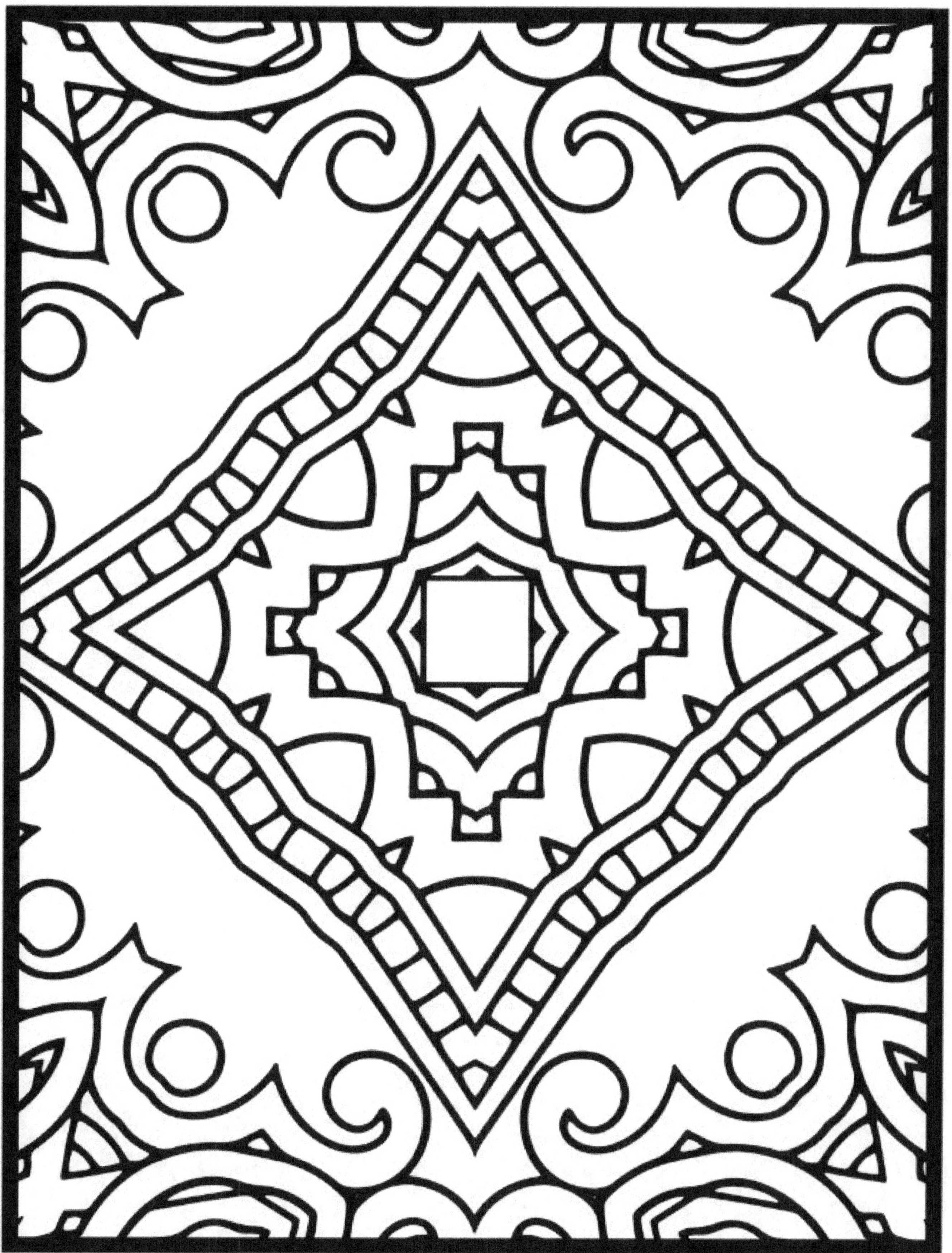

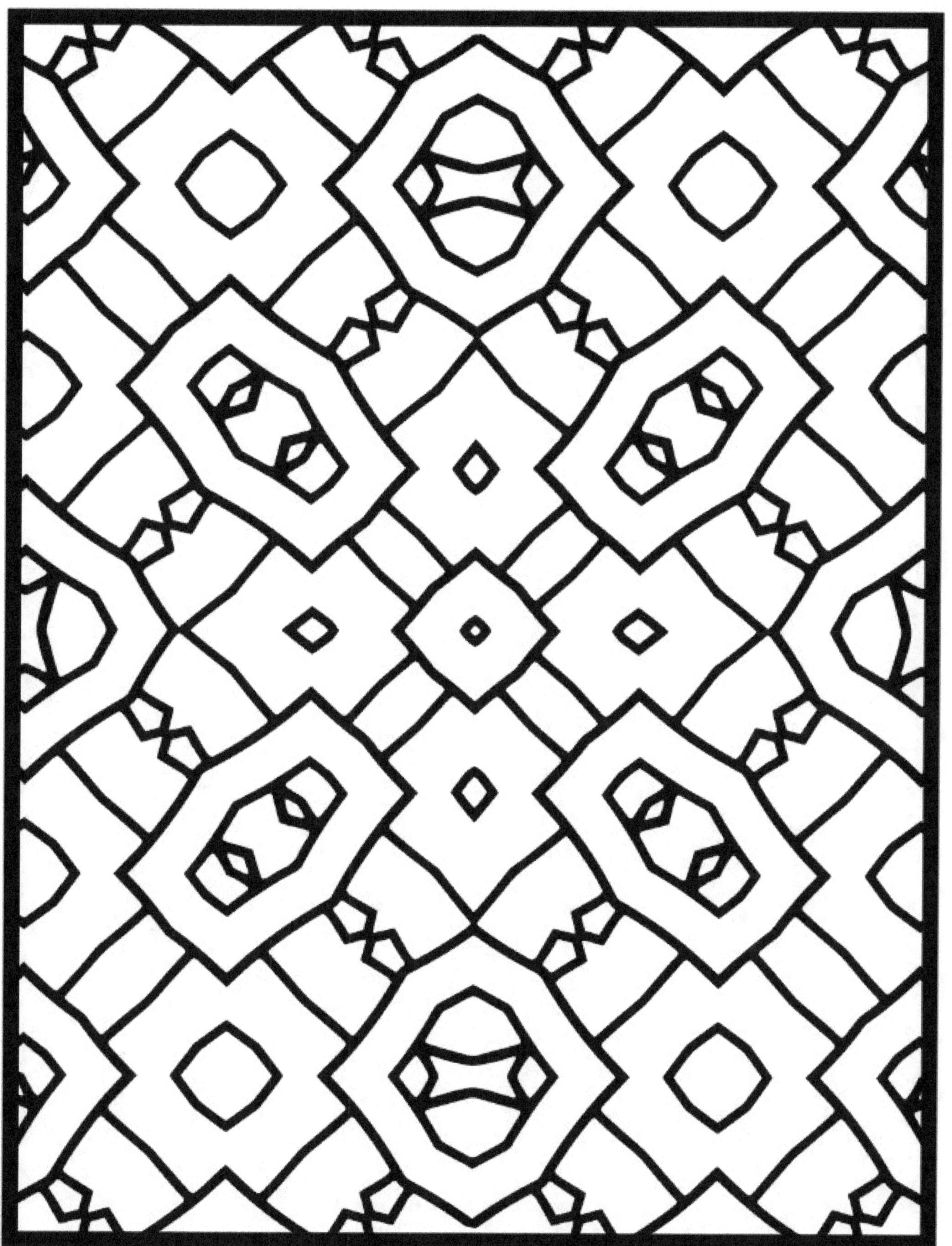

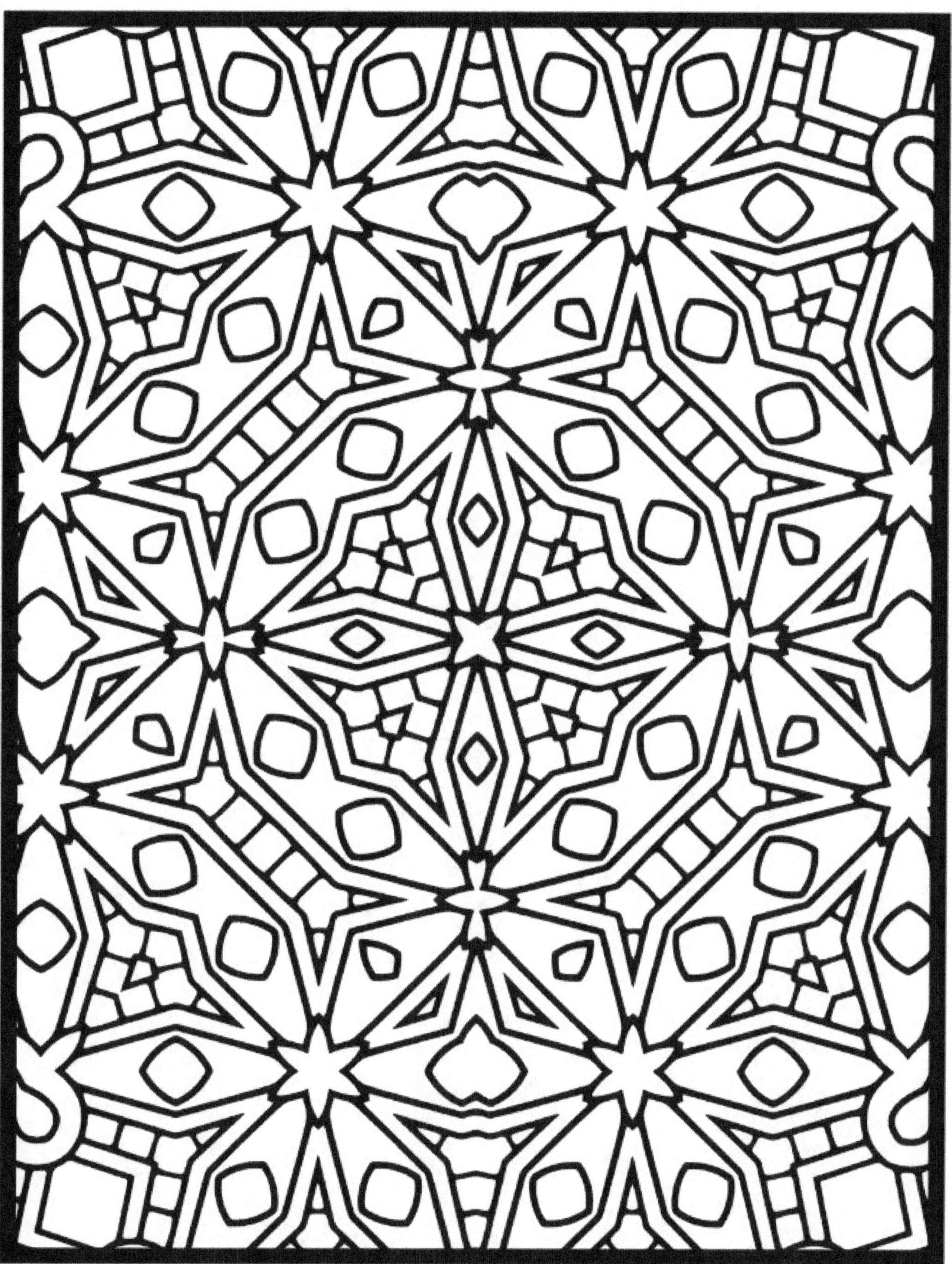

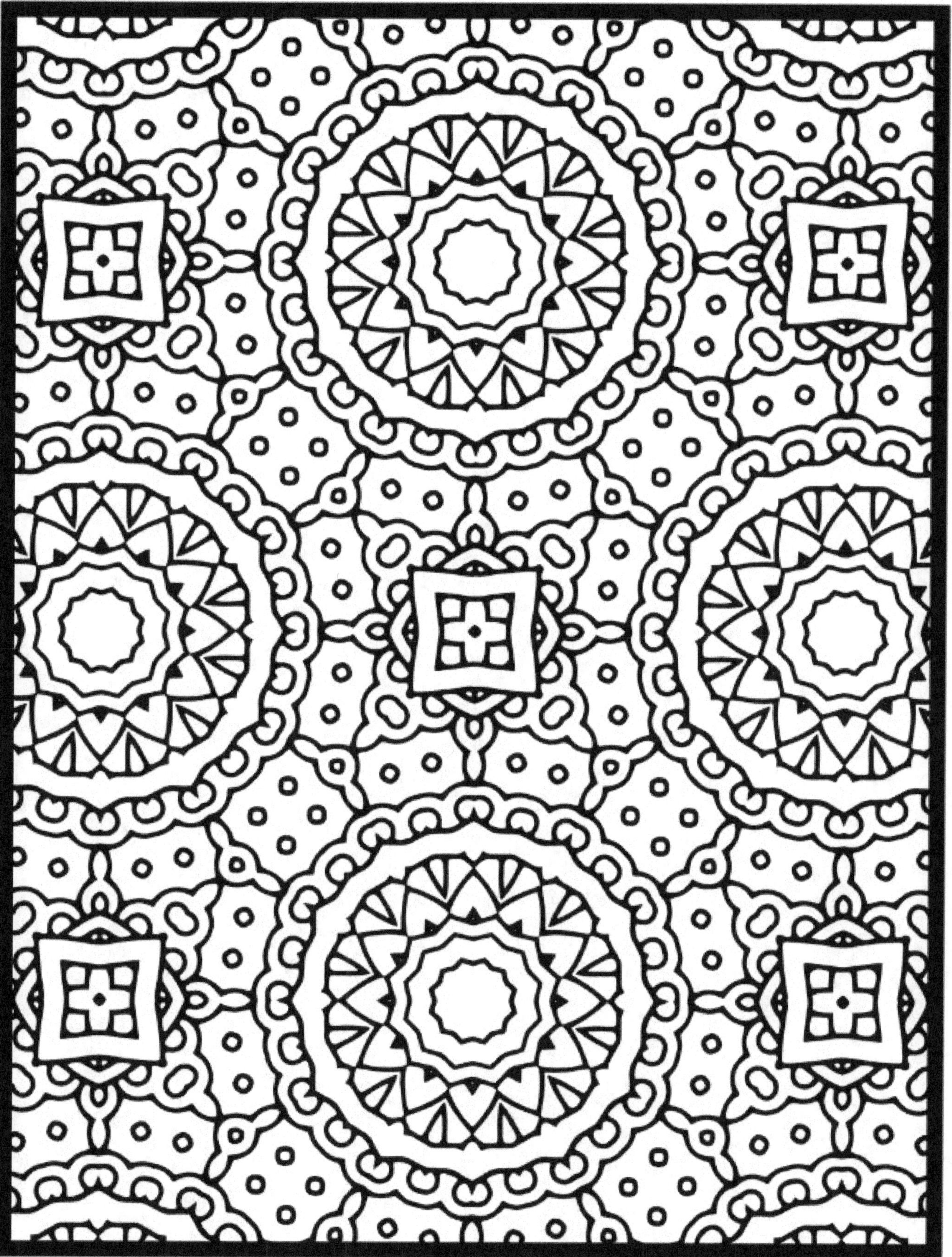

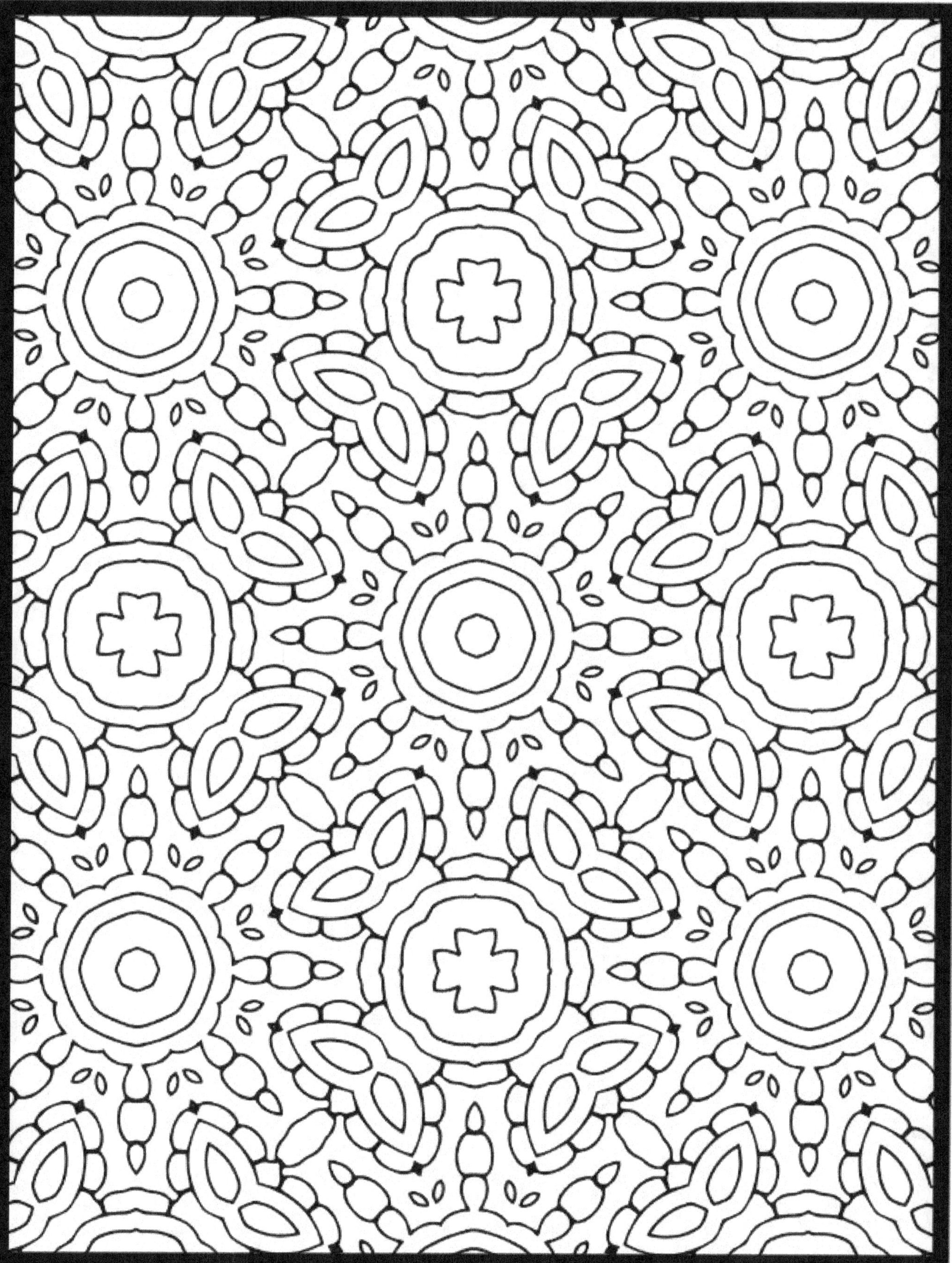

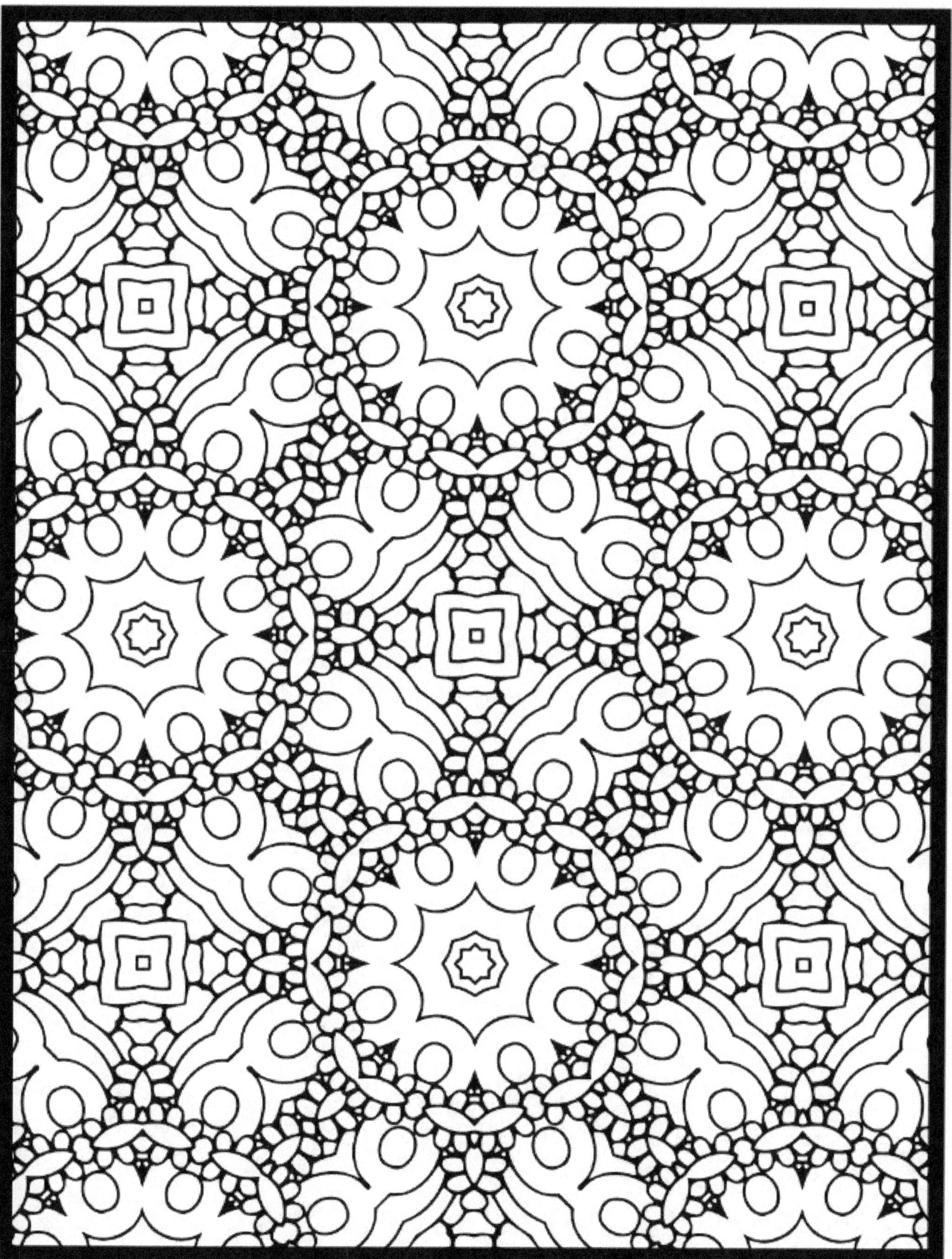

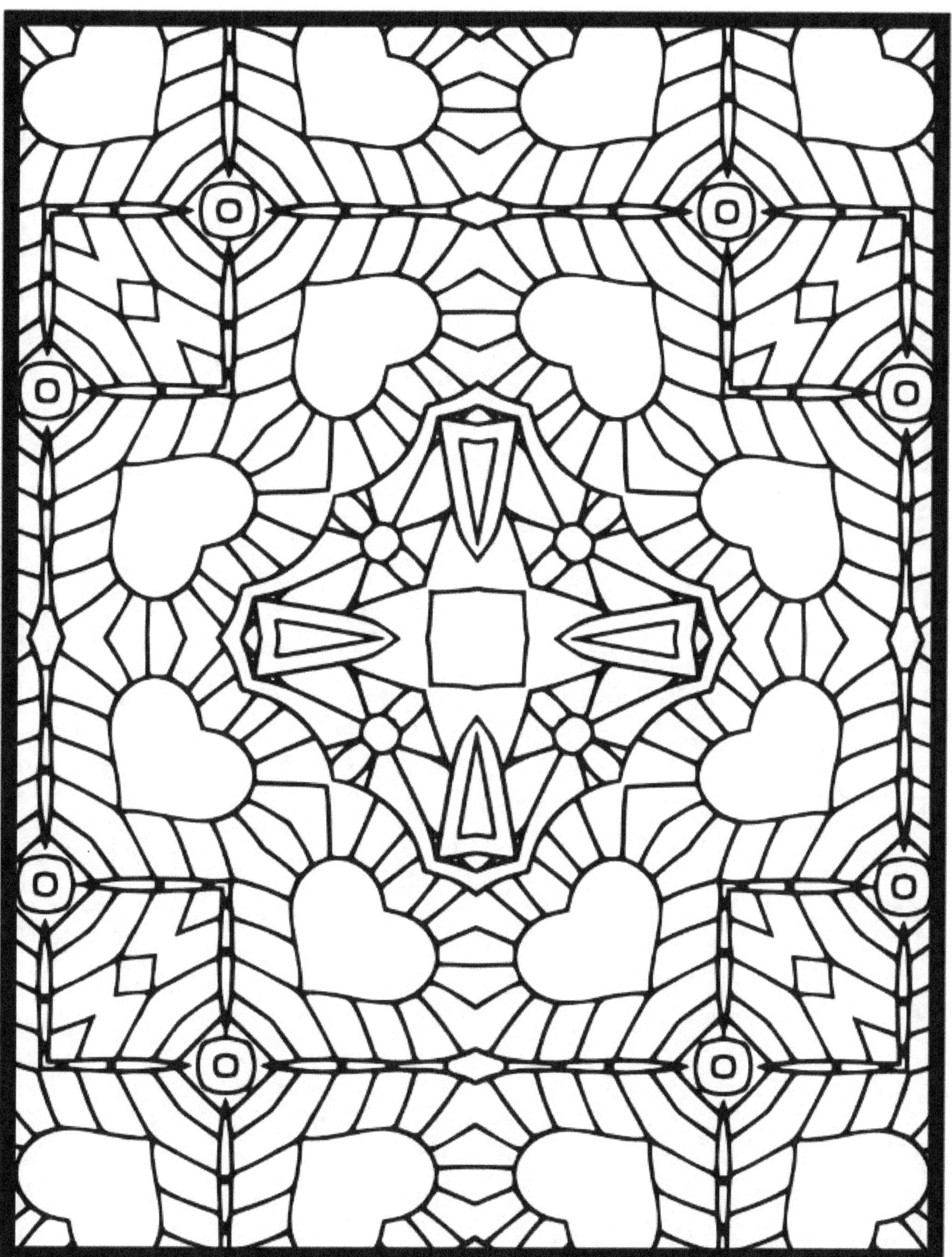

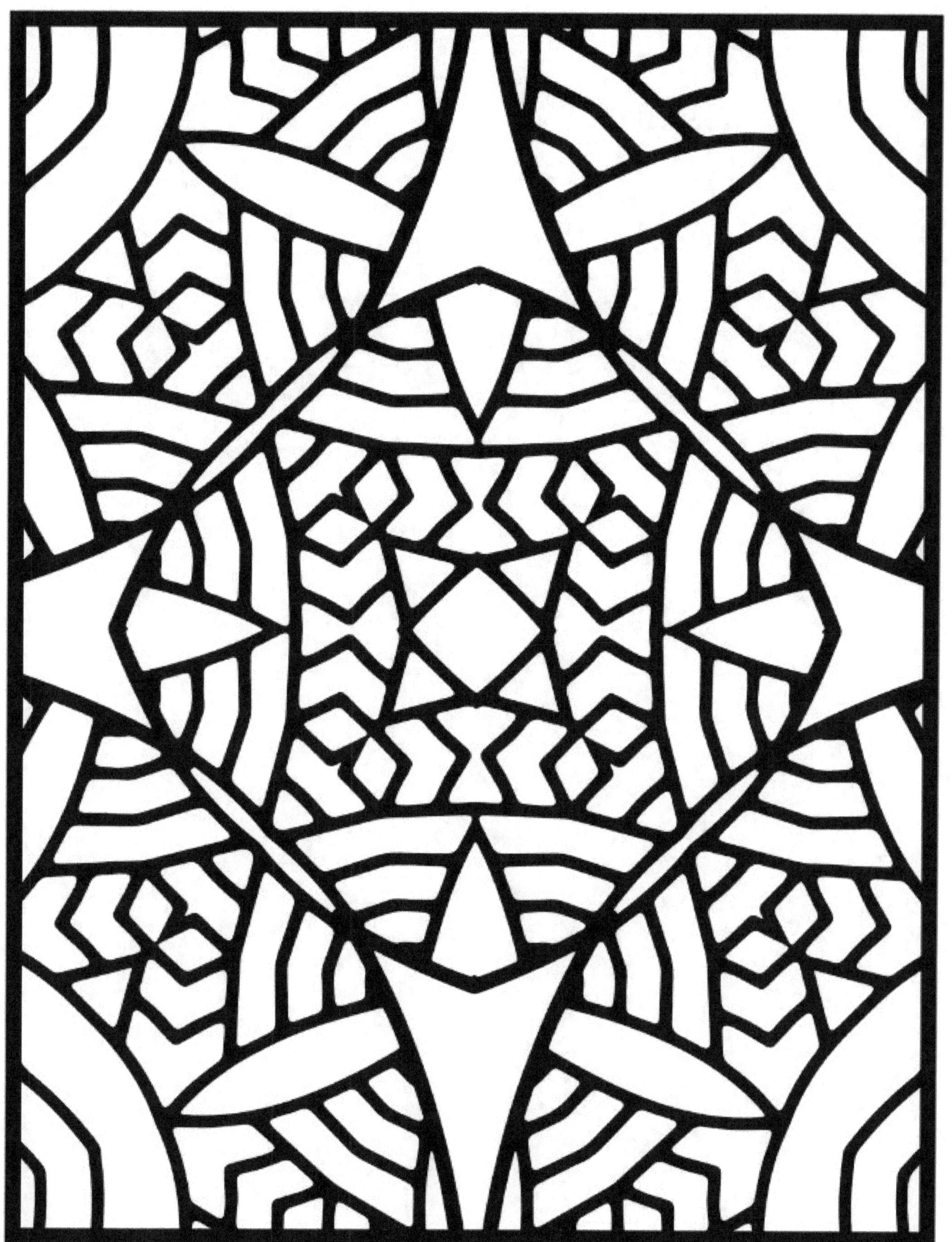

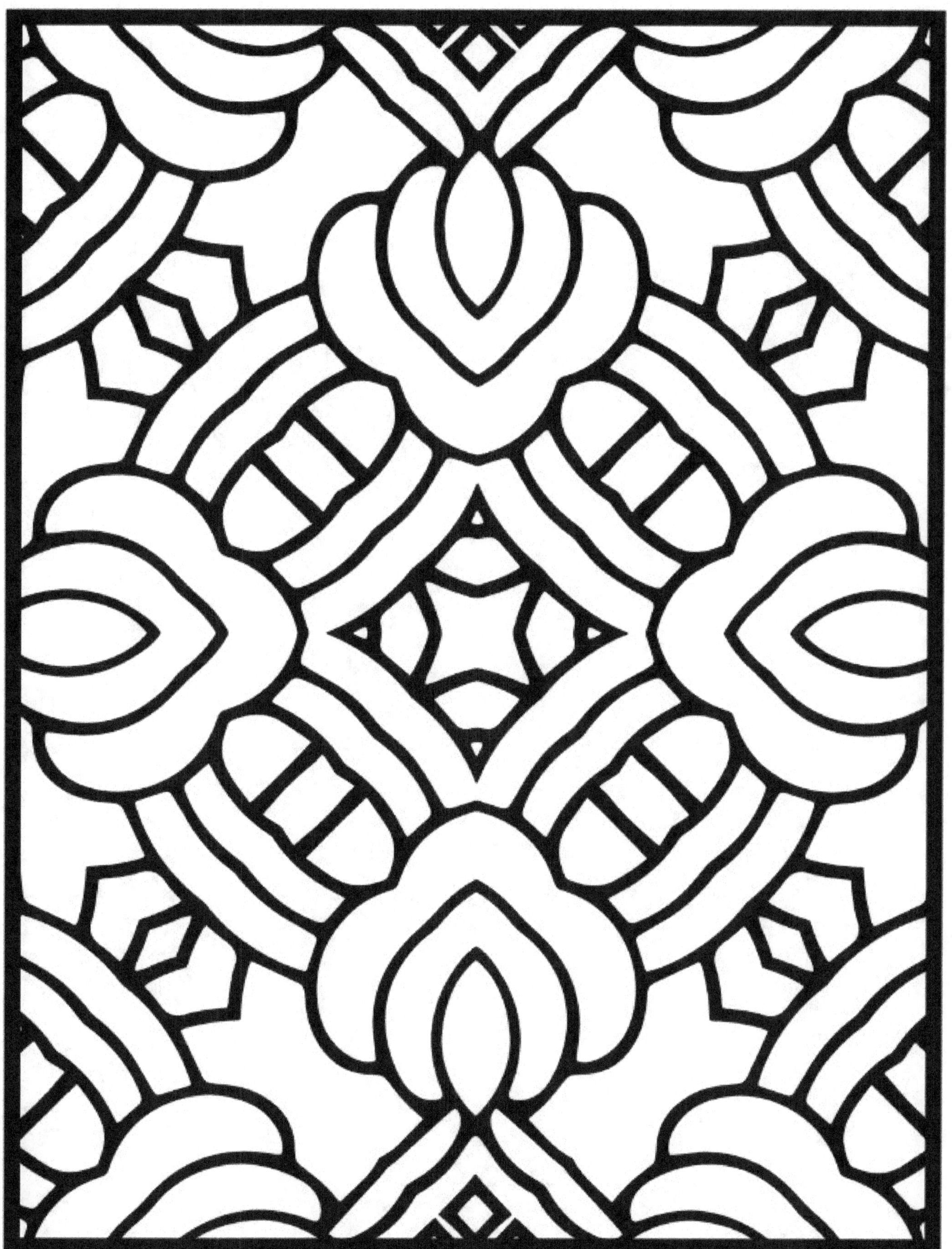

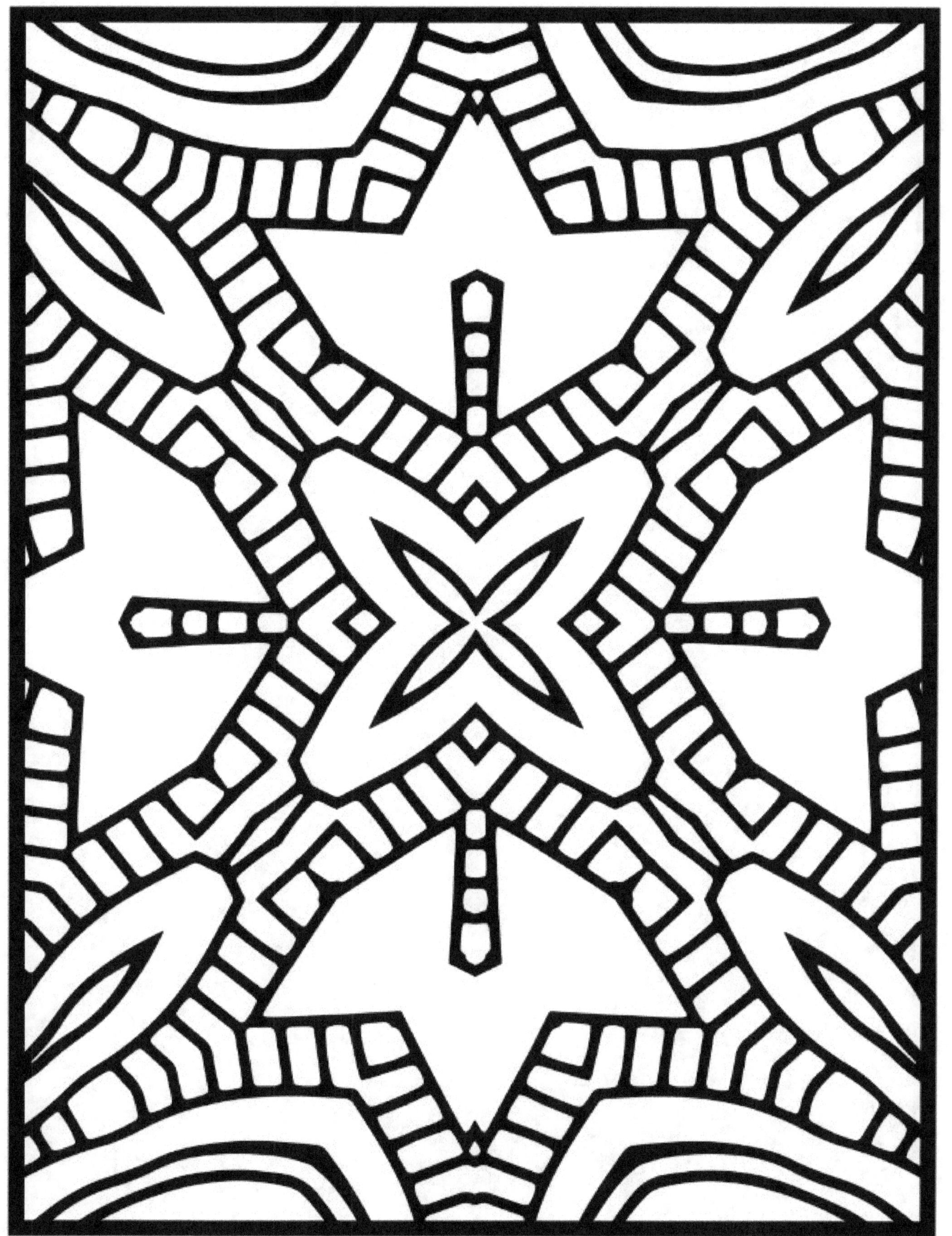

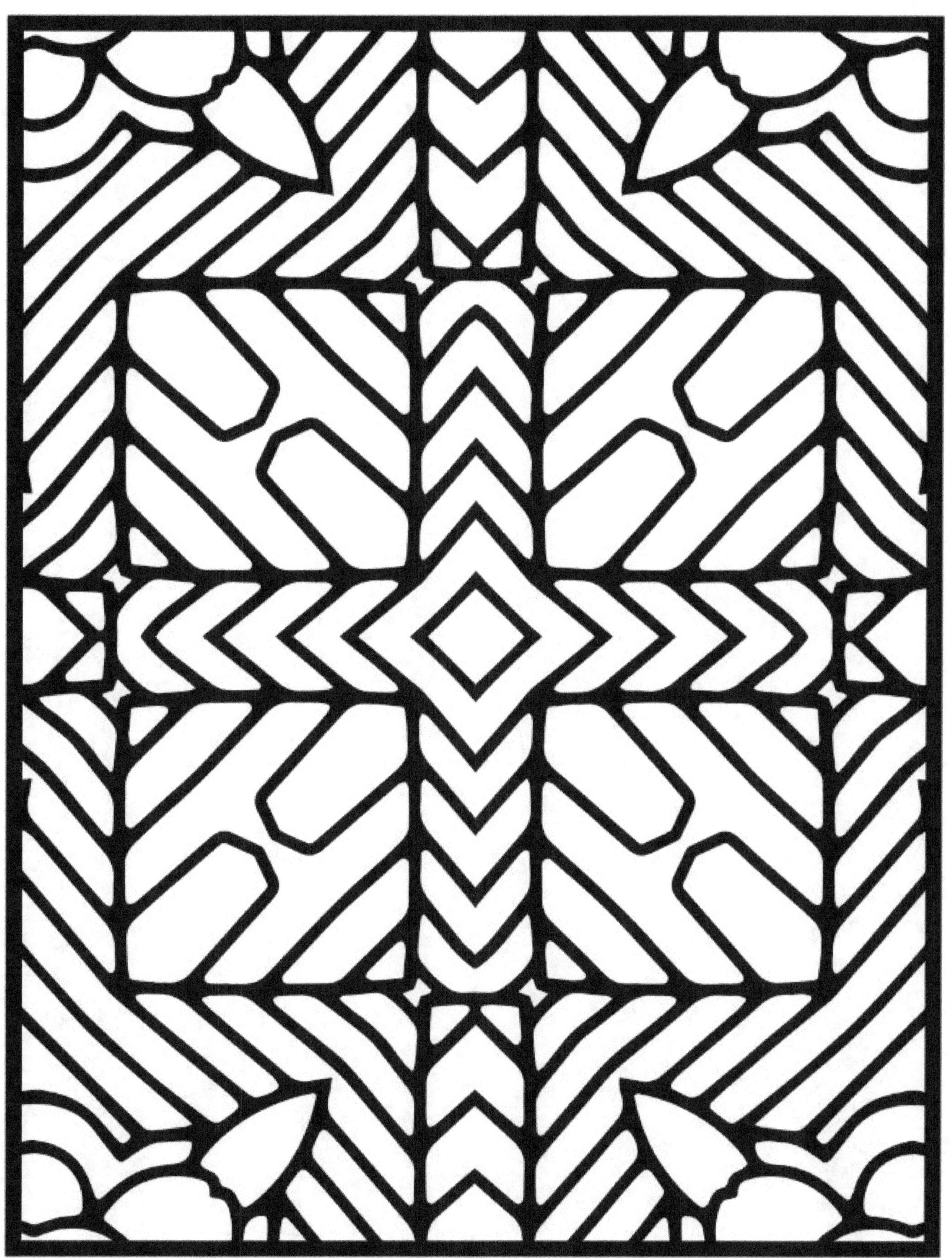

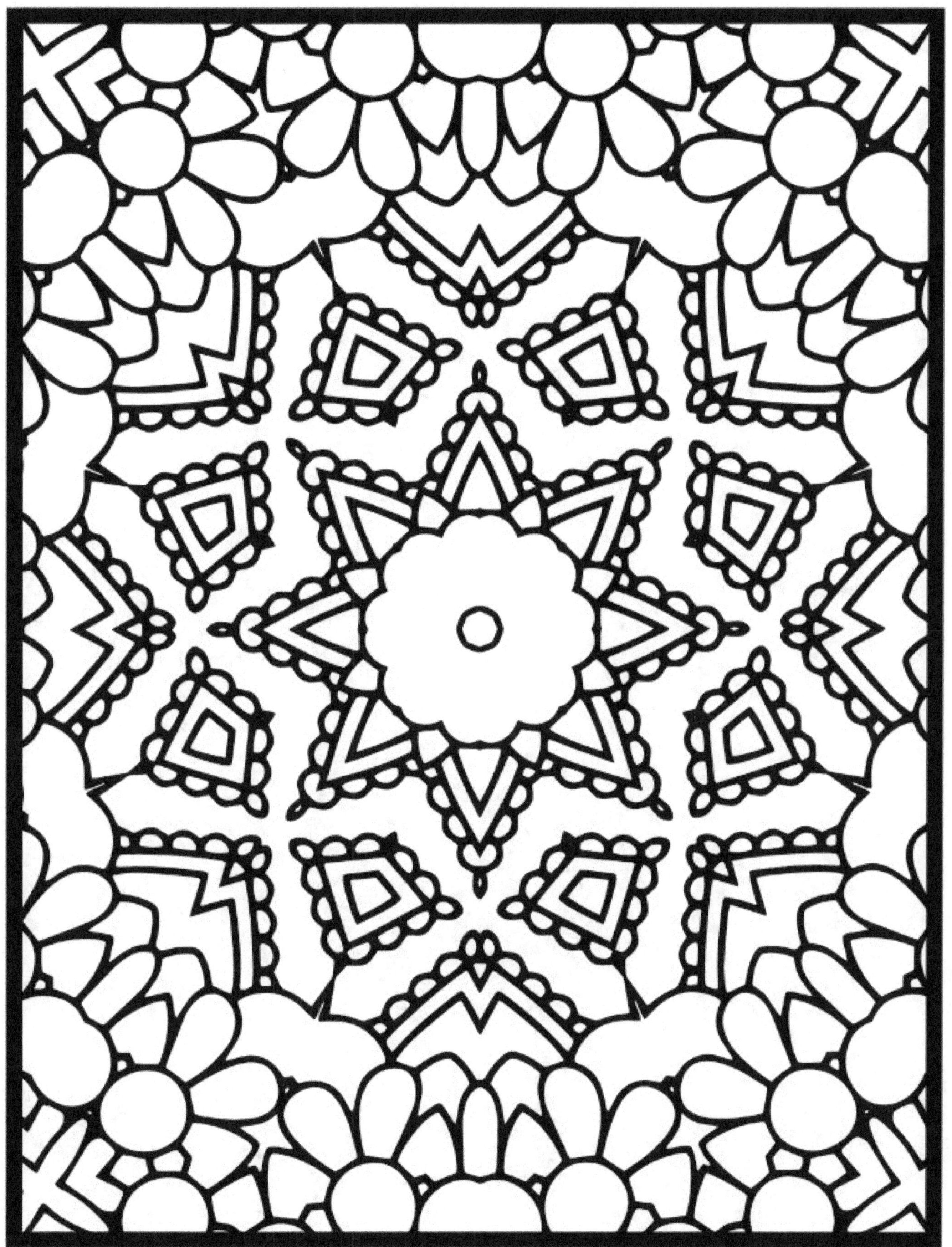

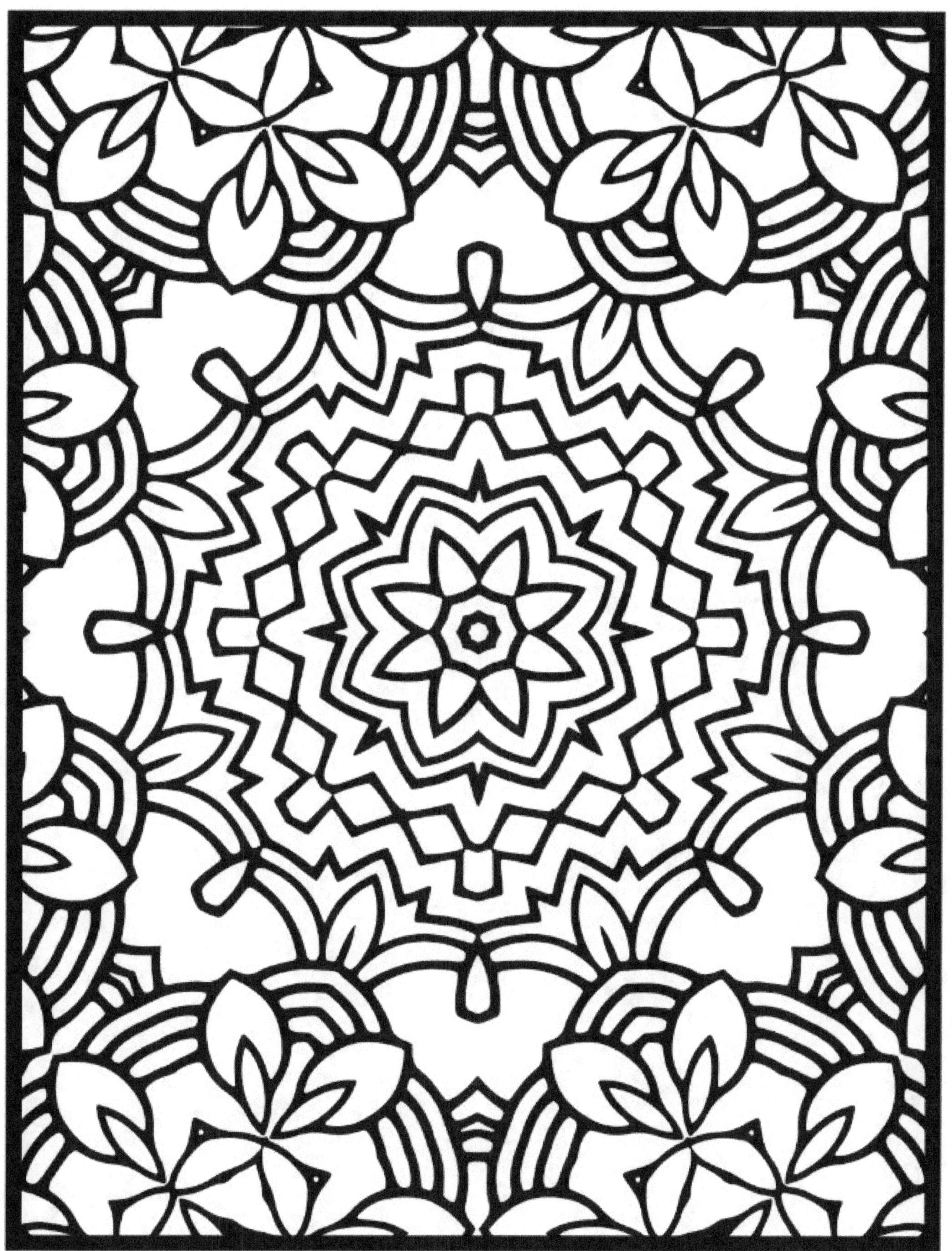

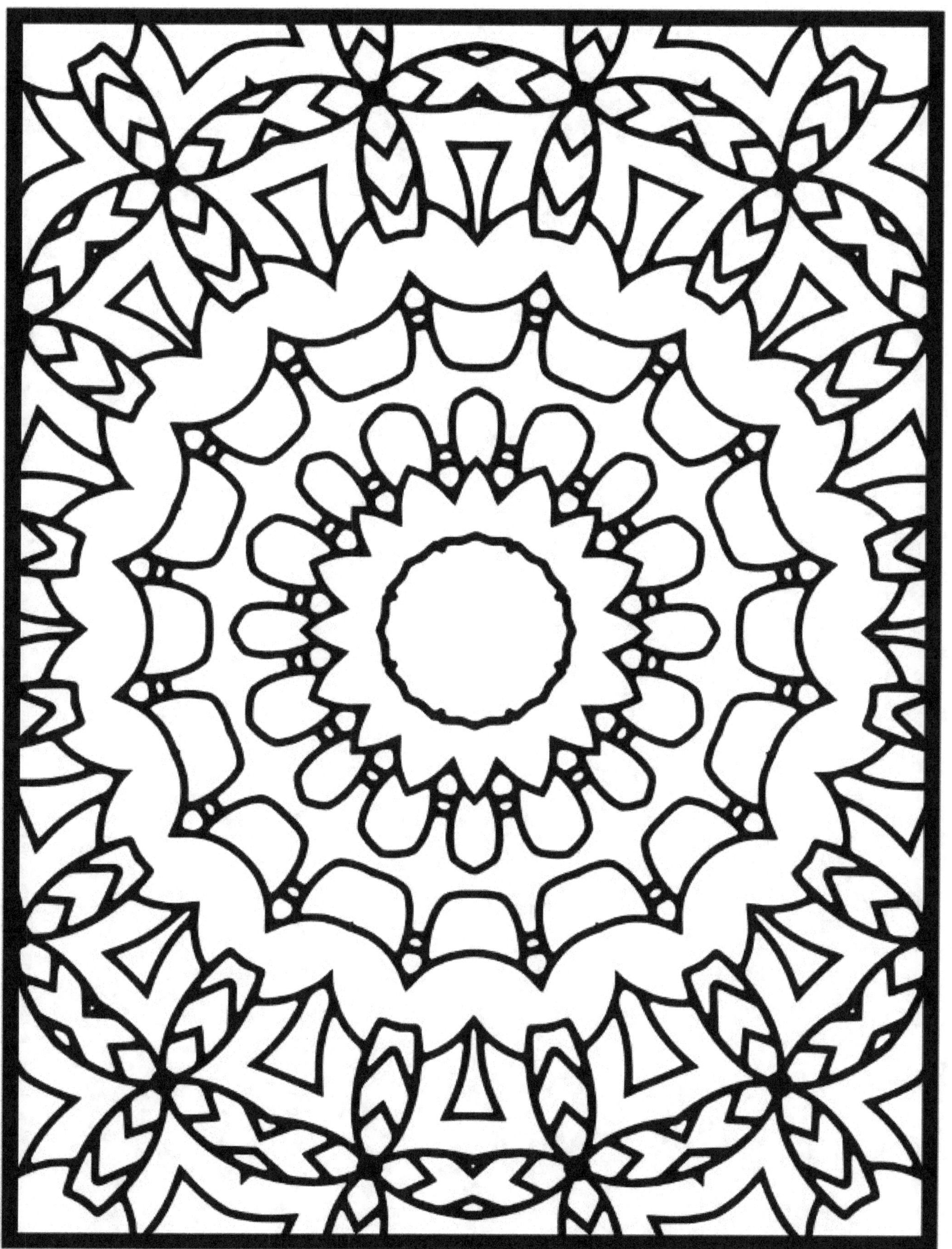

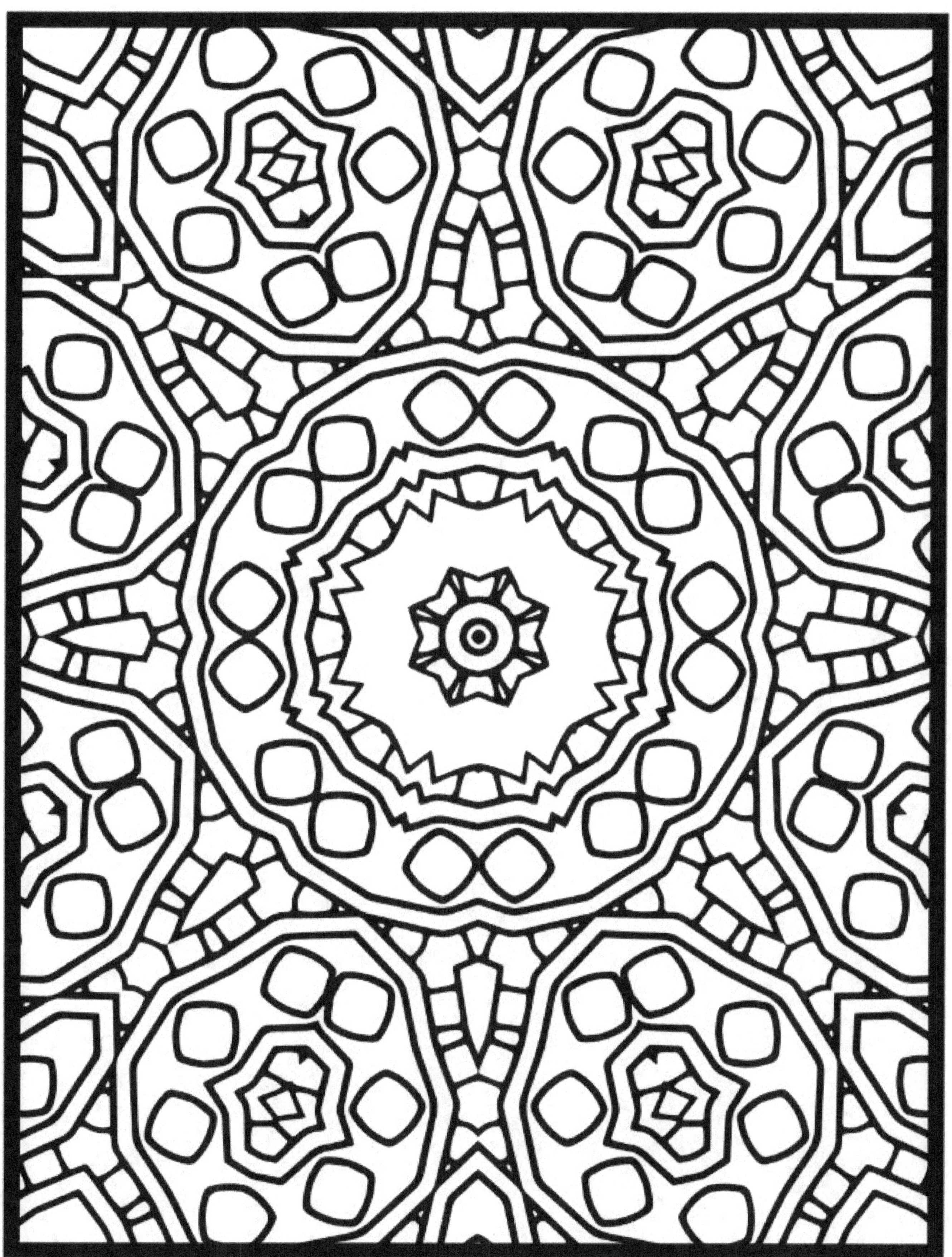

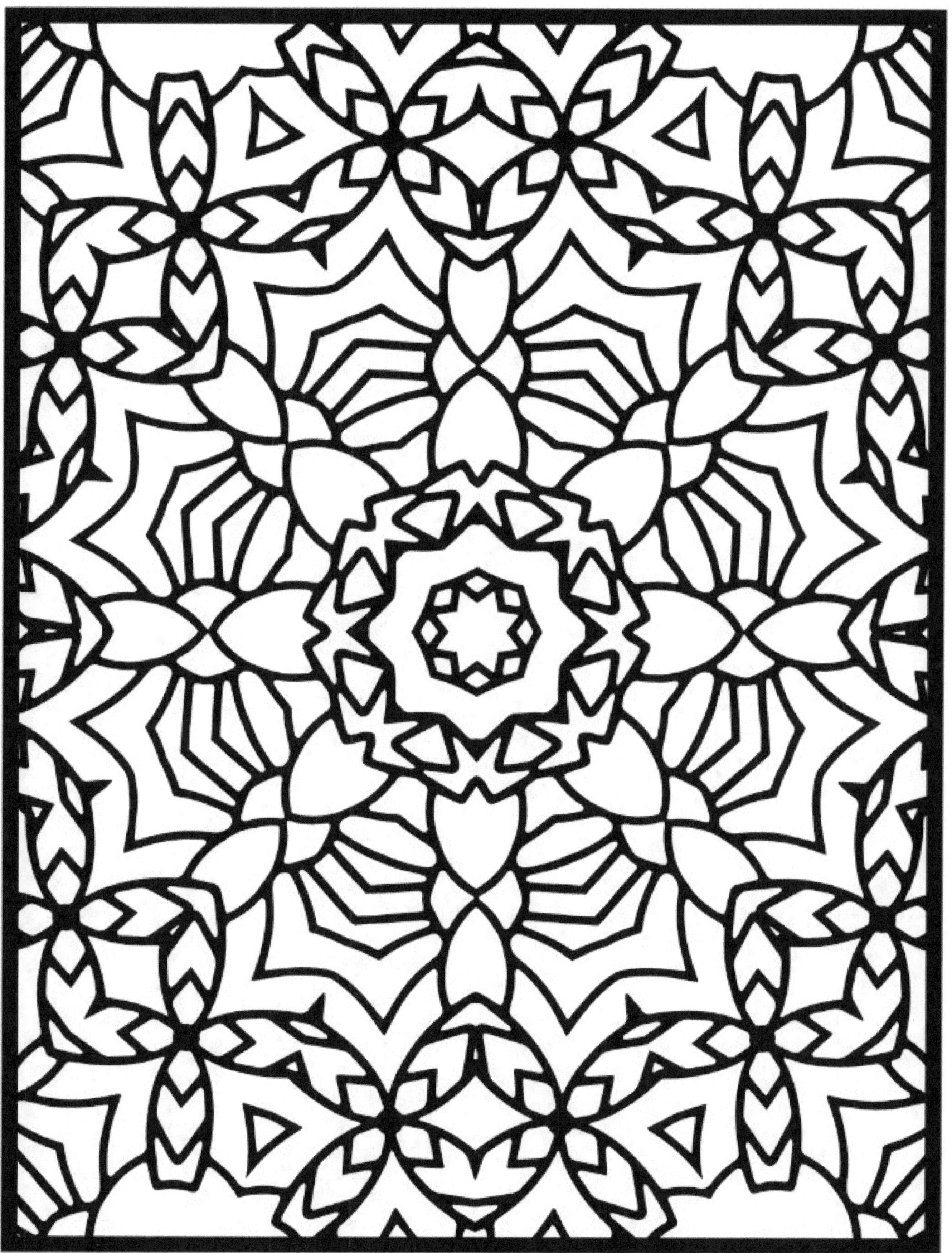

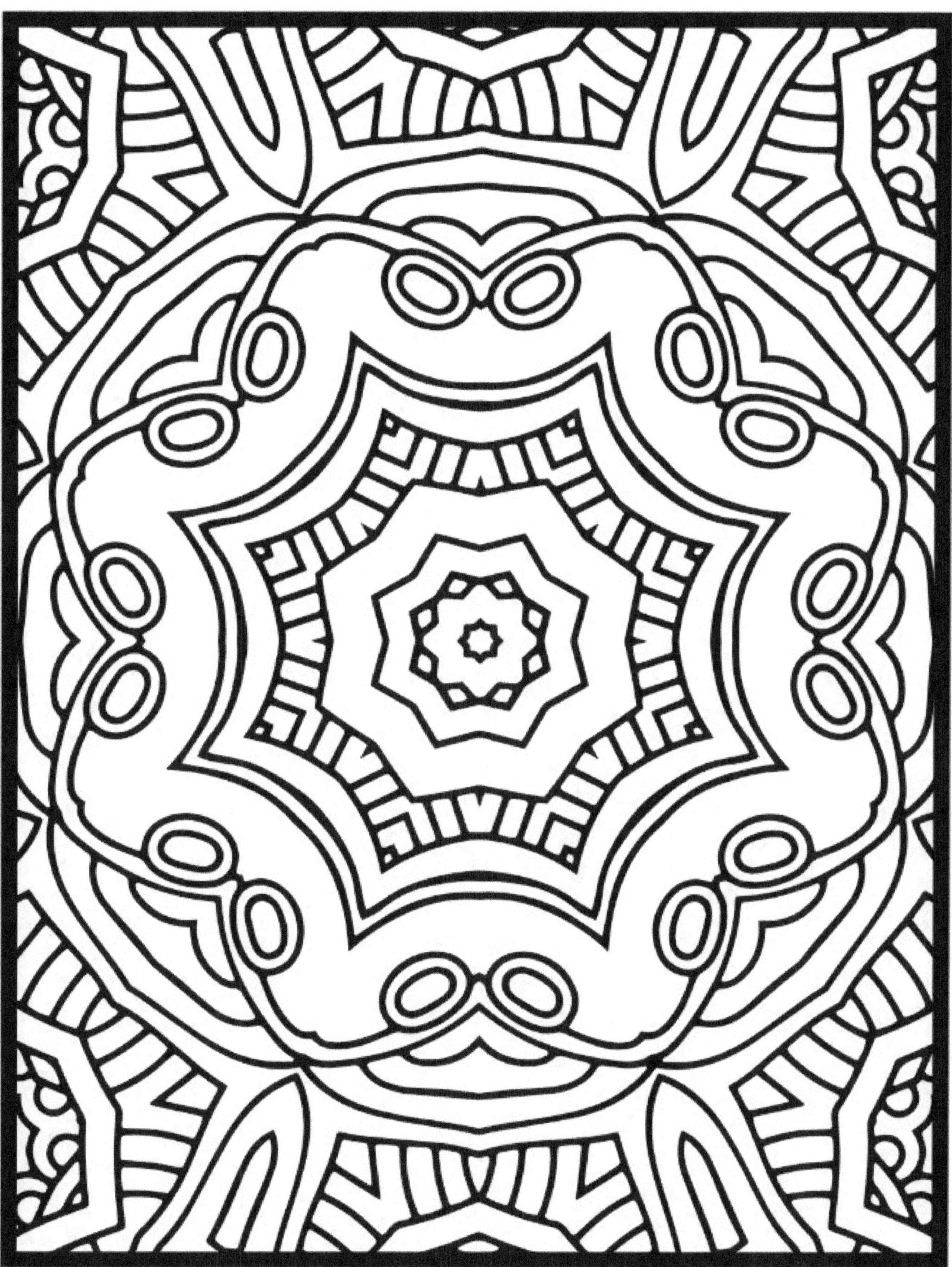

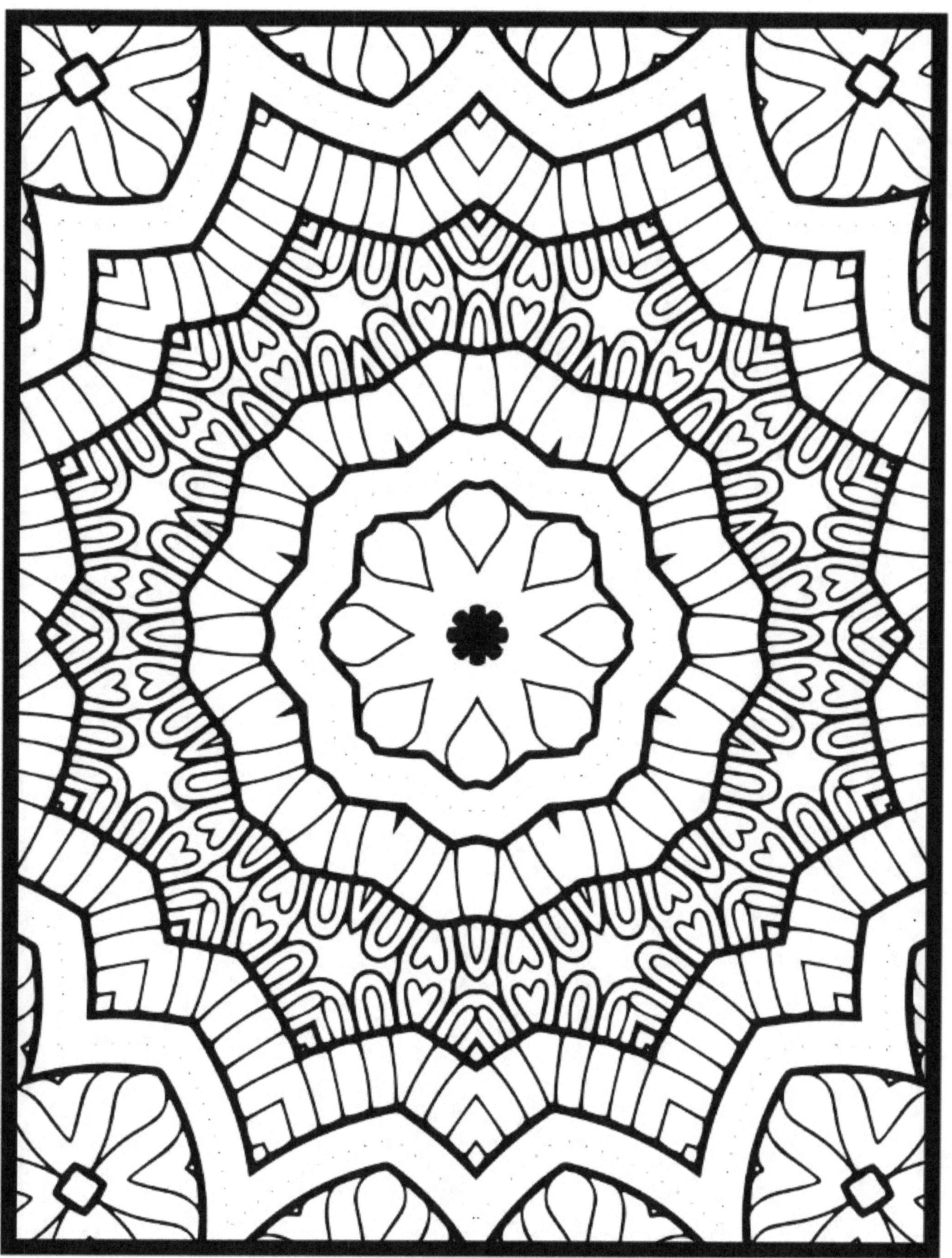

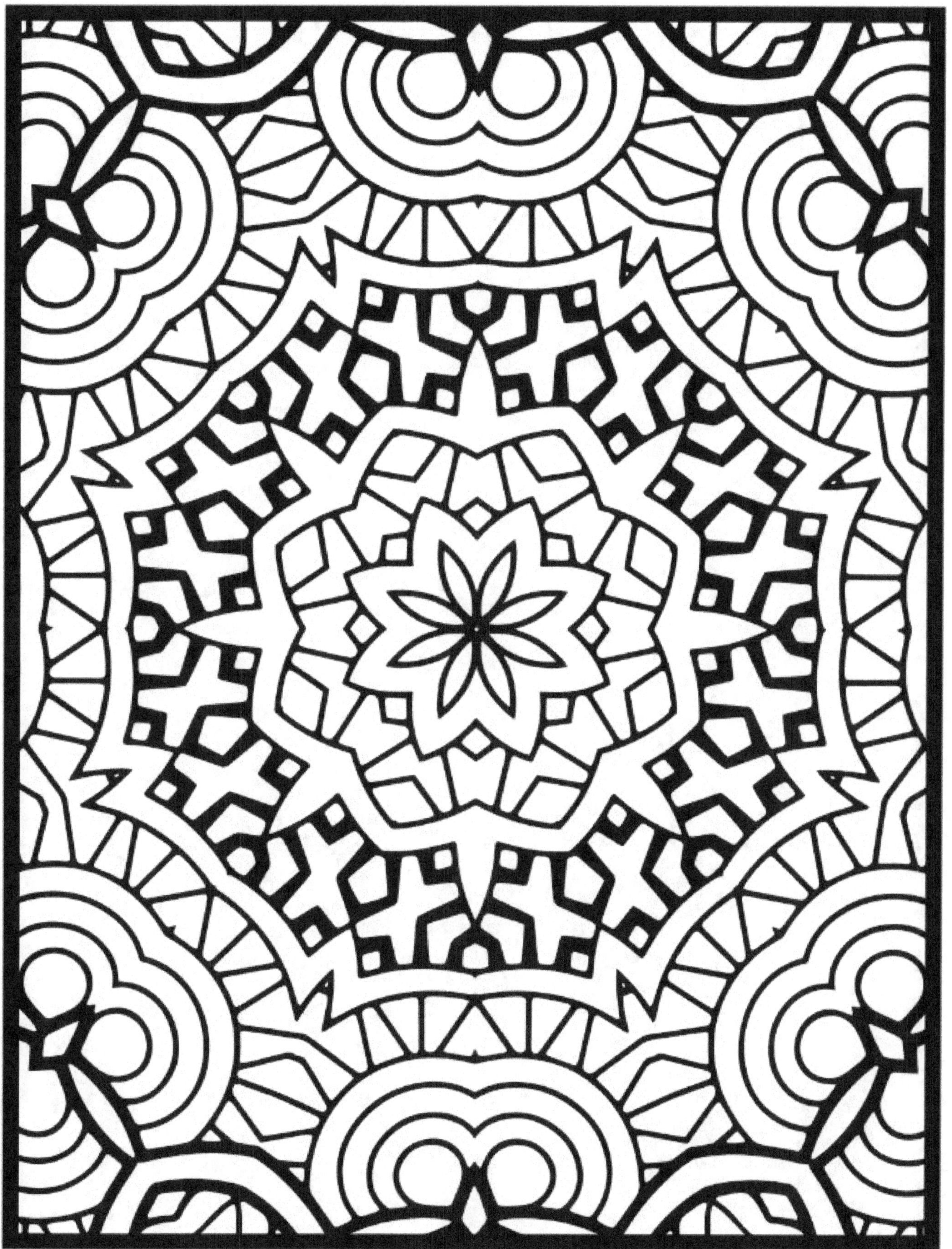

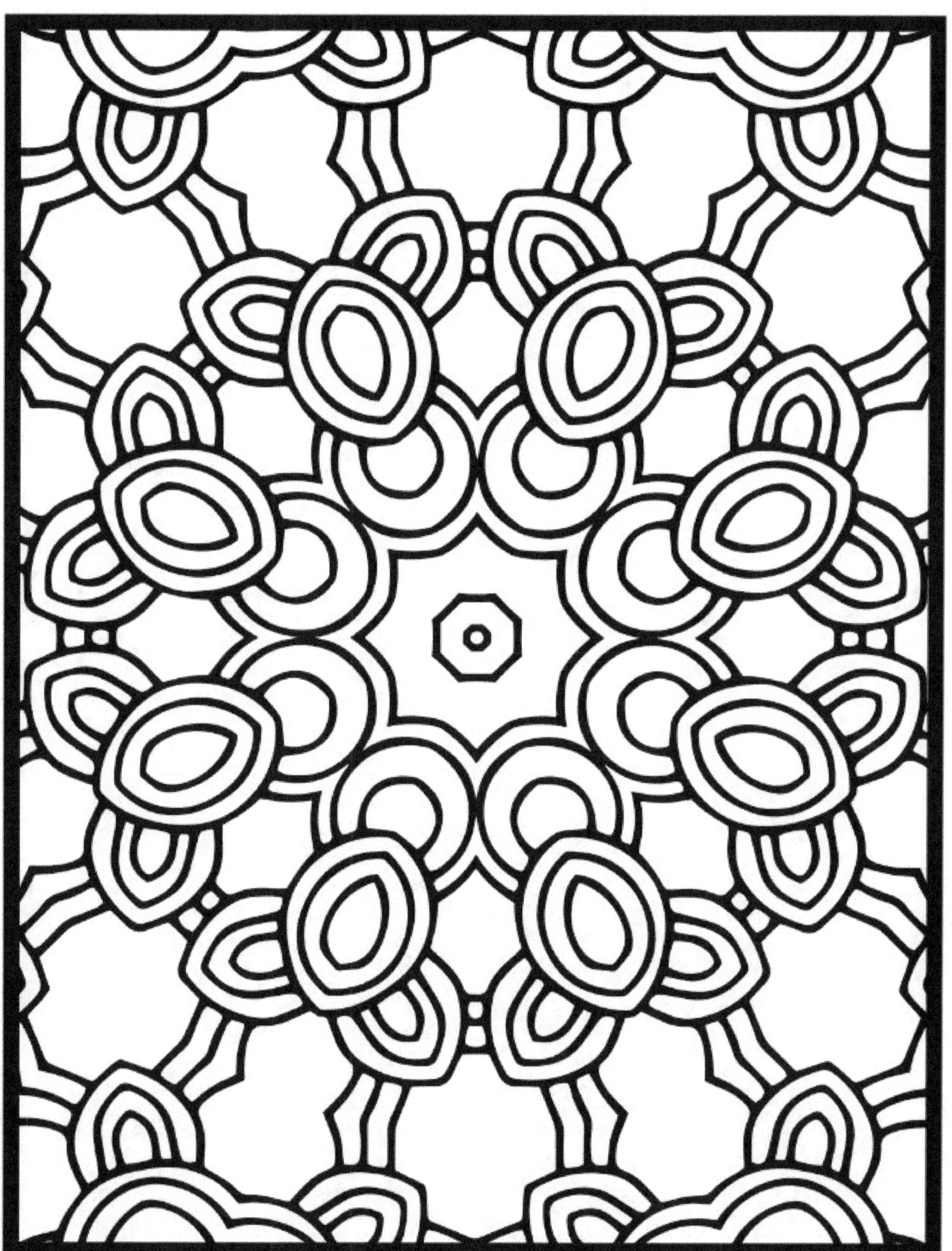

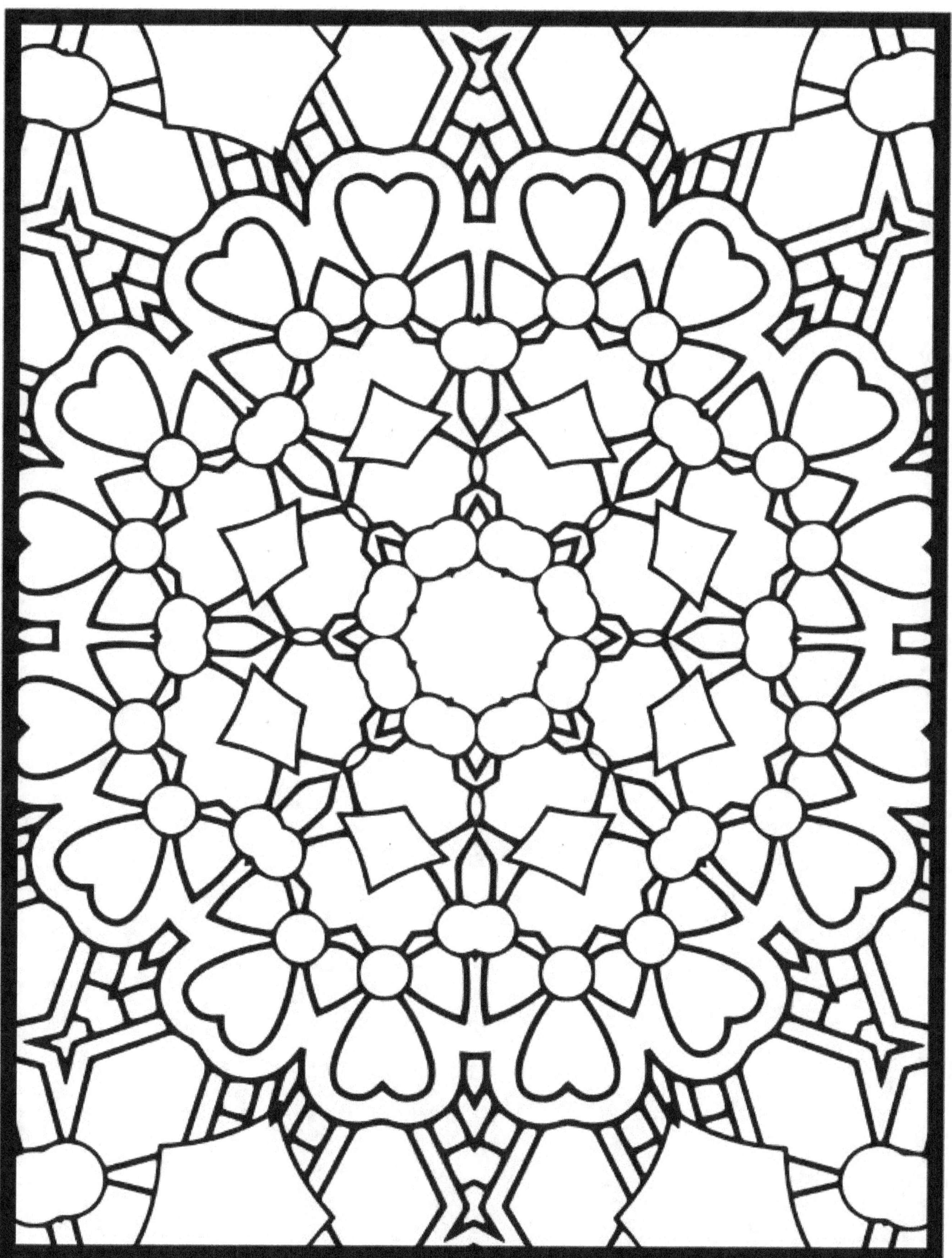

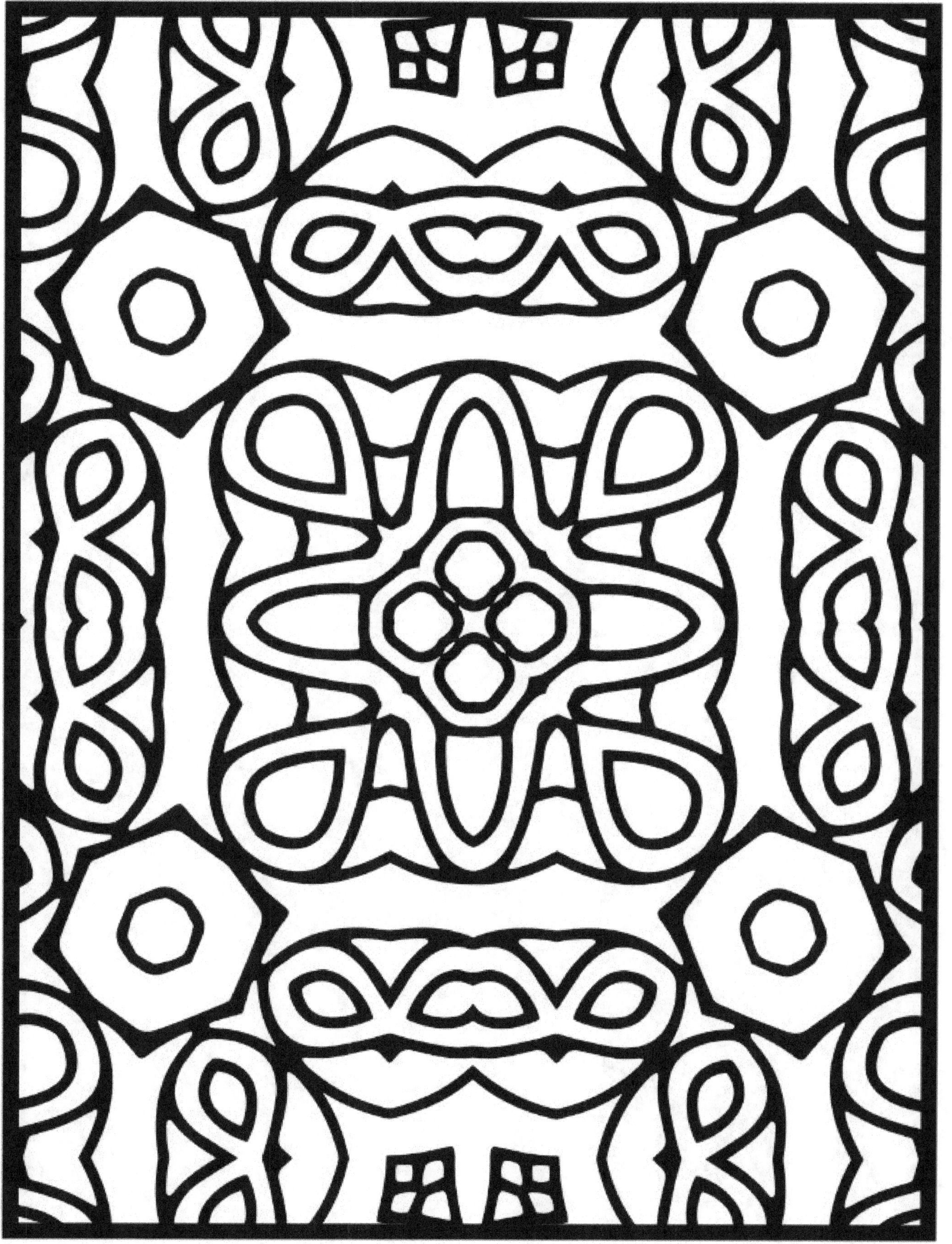

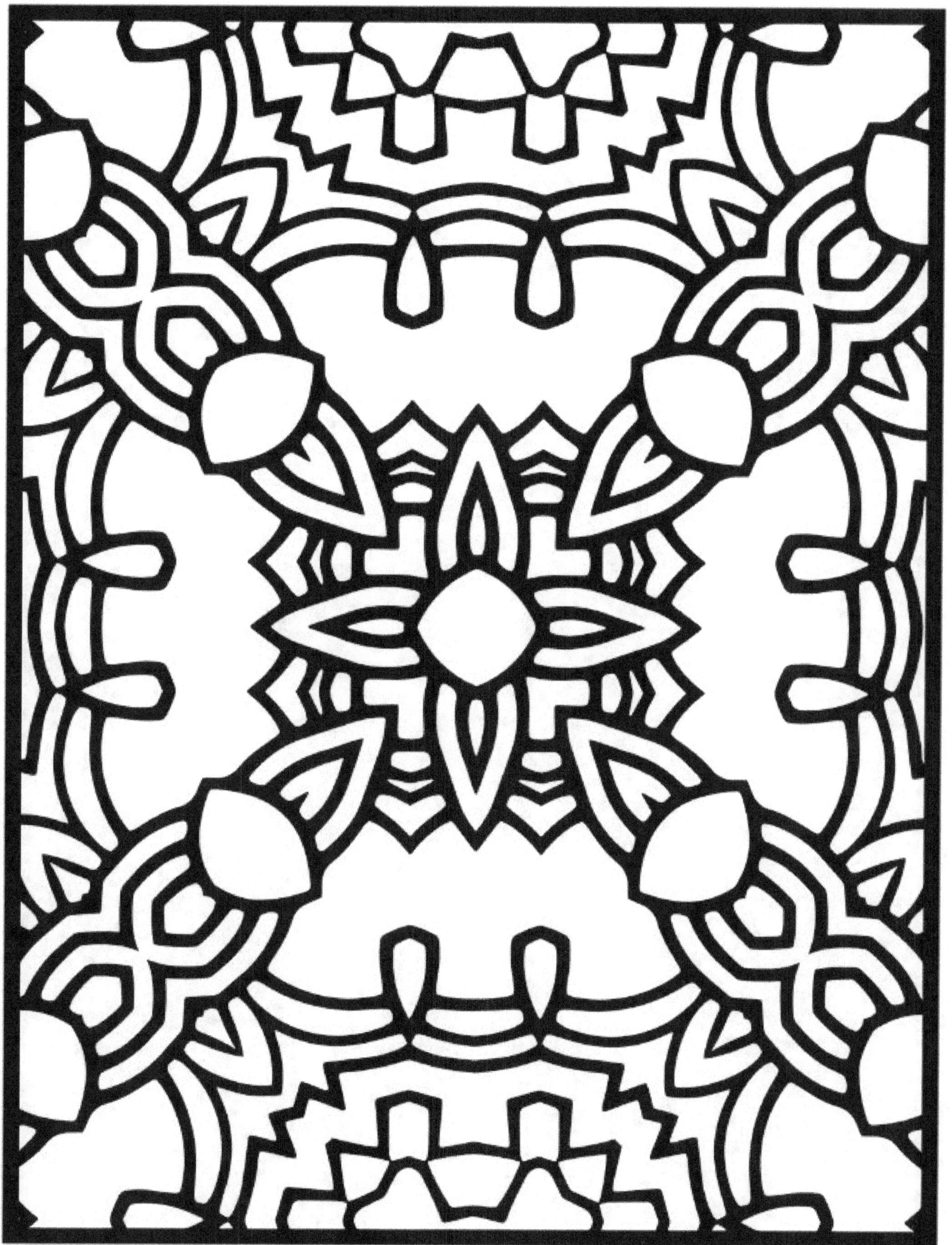

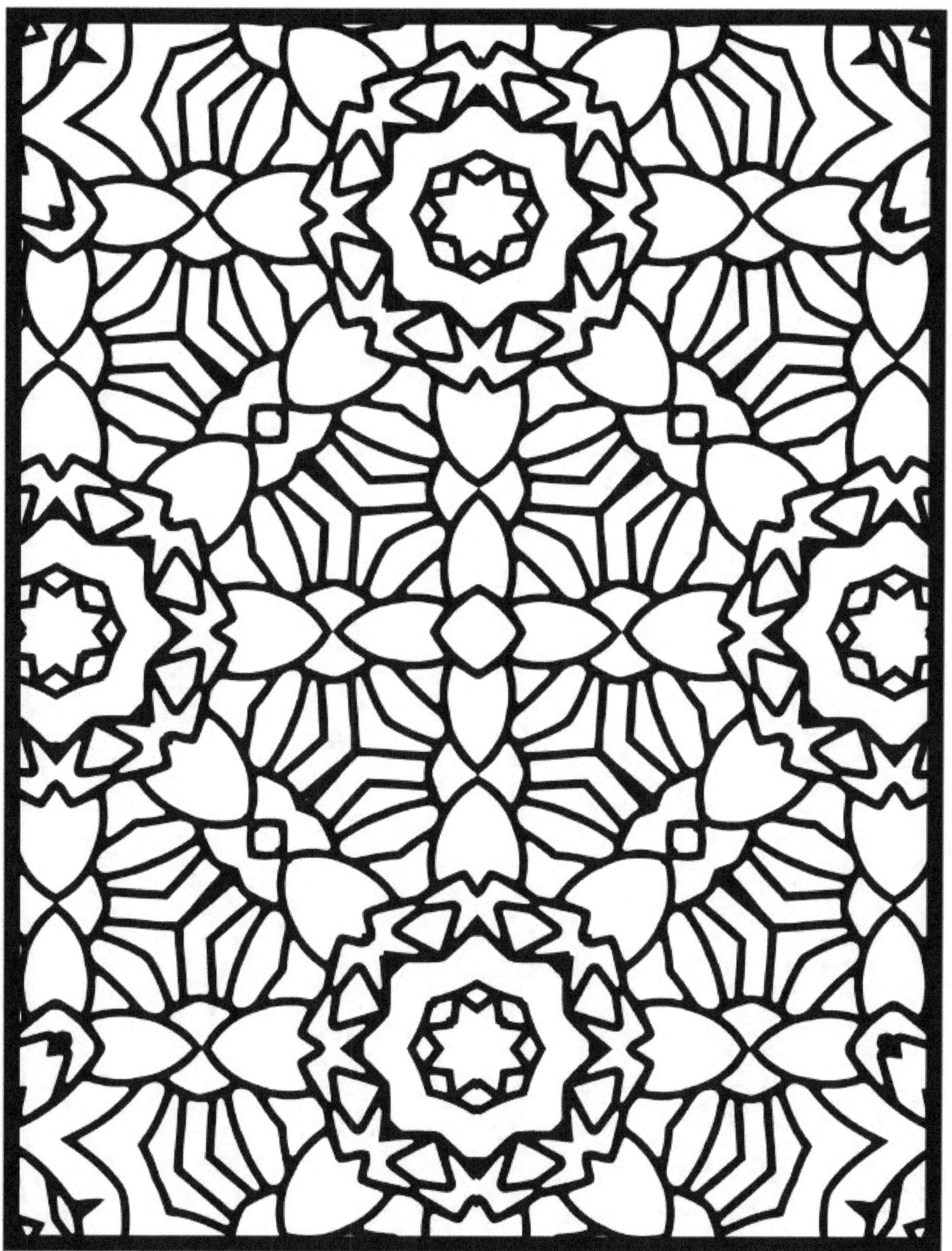

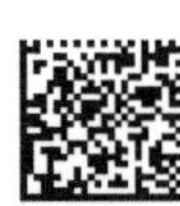